Palgrave Studies in Education and the Environment

Series Editors
Alan Reid
Faculty of Education
Monash University
Melbourne, VIC, Australia

Marcia McKenzie
College of Education
University of Saskatchewan
Saskatoon, SK, Canada

This series focuses on new developments in the study of education and environment. Promoting theoretically-rich works, contributions include empirical and conceptual studies that advance critical analysis in environmental education and related fields. Concerned with the underlying assumptions and limitations of current educational theories in conceptualizing environmental and sustainability education, the series highlights works of theoretical depth and sophistication, accessibility and applicability, and with critical orientations to matters of public concern. It engages interdisciplinary and diverse perspectives as these relate to domains of policy, practice, and research. Studies in the series may span a range of scales from the more micro level of empirical thick description to macro conceptual analyses, highlighting current and upcoming turns in theoretical thought. Tapping into a growing body of theoretical scholarship in this domain, the series provides a venue for examining and expanding theorizations and approaches to the interdisciplinary intersections of environment and education. Its timeliness is clear as education becomes a key mode of response to environmental and sustainability issues internationally. The series will offer fresh perspectives on a range of topics such as:

- curricular responses to contemporary accounts of human-environment relations (e.g., the Anthropocene, nature-culture, animal studies, transdisciplinary studies)
- the power and limits of new materialist perspectives for philosophies of education
- denial and other responses to climate change in education practice and theory
- place-based and land-based orientations to education and scholarship
- postcolonial and intersectional critiques of environmental education and its research
- policy research, horizons, and contexts in environmental and sustainability education

More information about this series at
http://www.palgrave.com/gp/series/15084

Malin Ideland

The Eco-Certified Child

Citizenship and Education for
Sustainability and Environment

Malin Ideland
Faculty of Education and Society
Malmö University
Malmö, Sweden

Palgrave Studies in Education and the Environment
ISBN 978-3-030-00198-8   ISBN 978-3-030-00199-5   (eBook)
https://doi.org/10.1007/978-3-030-00199-5

Library of Congress Control Number: 2018955456

An earlier version of the text in this book was published in Swedish with the title Den KRAV-märkta
människan (Celanders förlag 2016). Translated by Alan Crozier.

Cover illustration: © Melisa Hasan

This Palgrave Pivot imprint is published by the registered company Springer Nature Switzerland AG
The registered company address is: Gewerbestrasse 11, 6330 Cham, Switzerland

To my girls, Tova and Malva Ideland, whom I hope to be willing and able to hear and tell more than the single story.

Foreword

The Eco-Certified Child. Citizenship and Education for Sustainability and Environment brings into view paradoxes of the good intentions of schooling to provide for a more enlightened and progressive society. The paradoxes are embodied in the very efforts to provide a more inclusive, thoughtful and progressive society that simultaneously produces exclusions and abjections. The book provocatively engages today's doxa or commonsense about enacting the moral and social commitments of education through examining the principles that order what is said, thought about and done in the name of those good intentions.

The substance of the analysis focuses on Swedish environmental and sustainable development education. But the case is not about national programs and their particularities. The case is the very conditions of enactments that order and classify the desires of modern education. And in this case of paradox is how the fondness of science as the privileged knowledge for rectifying social wrongs is enacted in the school. Ideland's study illuminates how what is named as science is a translation and transmogrification in the curriculum as cultural theses about modes of living. I use the plural—cultural theses about modes of living—to refer to a continuum of values that differentiates the sustainable child from the child cast as different and excluded as "unstainable"! Sustainable development integrates the science and science education with economics and social education. This brings clearly into focus the curriculum as a cultural practice and the political of schooling. Educating about the appropriation/misappropriation natural recourses is about kinds of people that exclude and abject particular populations from equal participation in the name of rectifying social wrongs.

Let me start then with a general proposition about schooling that this book artfully and systematically brings into focus. The good intentions of the modern school continually connect with the hope of the European Enlightenment's cosmopolitanism, and with the faith in reason and science in producing a better and more rational and open-minded world.[1] Of course, the French *Philosophés*, *Republic of Letters* and *Encyclopédie*, did not talk about sustainable development. But they sought to applied *reason* as a critical eye to the society and its weakness in order to think about human betterment. These searches for progress were (re)visioned in the political theories of new republicanism and the formation of the modern, mass schooling of the nineteenth century.

What is important in this 'history' for understanding the significant contribution of Ideland's book is twofold. First, the Enlightenment's cosmopolitanism that emphasized a particular kind of person whose reason and rationality (science) was cast as models in the new republican forms of government. The new American and French republican governments of the

---

[1] Of course, the book and my discussion relate particularly to schools in Western Europe and North America. Yet my reference to the Enlightenment is not to colonialize the emergence of the modern school through universalizing and essentializing the Enlightenment. Rather, it is to recognize it as a space within particular historical formations that circulated internationally in different time/spaces. Marx was influenced by the Enlightenment, and the various forms of Marxism in the twentieth and twenty-first centuries are exemplars of this notion of travel as a relation and historical concept. For example, the marvel of John Dewey's pragmatism in the United States was to provide a way to bring Enlightenment's cosmopolitan values into the everyday organization of schooling; but the traveling of Dewey's ideas as they moved into China and Turkey, for example, were not merely copies of the cultural principles enunciated in the pragmaticism. What is assembled and connected (and disconnected) are not merely copies or borrowing to make the new schools, which requires unthinking and rethinking historical differentiations without inserting binaries such as the West and "Other". (See, e.g., Popkewitz, 2005; Popkewitz, Khursid, & Zhao, 2014)

nineteenth century as well as in Sweden by the end of that century, were depended on particular historically derived rationalities about the wisdom of the citizen, as evident in today's European and American debates about multicultural and intercultural education. The notions of the rational individual historically connected collective norms of belonging with those of civic responsibilities to participate in the society made possible governing and contributing in the social progress. If we think about the American Declaration of Independence (1776) calling for the purpose of government as "Life, Liberty, and the Pursuit of Happiness" and the French "Declaration of the Rights of the Man and of the Citizen" (1789), these are radical phrases not only about the natural right of people to freedom but also the governing of the kind of person who inhabits the spaces of participation.

Schooling became a central site for the making of this kind of person necessary for the intricacies of social life and government. The citizen is one that continually needs to be made, as it is not born as such. It entails a different subjectivity that the person is the subject of a sovereign. The person is spoken about in social and educational theories as one whose modes of life enable freedom, empowerment, participation, and collaboration to make possible the equitable and just societies, in which "eco-certified" child as a kind of person is central to this argument about environmental education and sustainable development. *What counts as the education for sustainable development, if I pursue this in Ideland's study is the inscription ofdiscoursesof sciences that are assembled and connected with cultural discourses of the wisdom of the citizen through the school curriculum.*

This brings me to the second element that provides an important contribution of this book for understanding the paradoxes of modern schooling. By the end of the nineteenth century, the distinction between reason (wisdom) and rationality mostly disappeared as the two notions are subsumed under the singular term of science. Science, then, became a social and cultural term that was not merely about particular kinds of expertise and what people do as scientists. Science becomes sets of historical principles for ordering, classifying and giving truth claims to what is seen, talked about and done in daily life. It is these different meanings of science that become ensconced in the school curriculum that is not merely the provenance of science education. The epistemic principles that connect the knowledge-content of "science" with pedagogical practices found in mathematics, music, and art education as well. The enactments of environmental and sustainable development give symbolic privilege to science but in fact whose name connects various sets of principles for ordering, classifying and governing in the making of kinds of people.

The focus on education for sustainable development and ecology becomes the cultural artifact investigated and the paradoxes of good intentions explored in this book. When I speak of science, it is to think about it as a cultural artifact that circulates in the school curriculum rather than as what people do in disciplinary fields and their production of knowledge.

First, science "acts" as the sacred knowledge of modernity. Science, since the nineteenth century, assumed cultural significance as the apotheosis of wisdom (Nye, 1999). Its knowledge had utopic qualities. It was to provide salvation and redemption through identifying the pathways to progress and human happiness. The inscription of science as a social knowledge captures, in one sense, the good intentions of sustainable development in the curriculum. In its contemporary terms, the faith in science turns to the particular trust given to positivism and empiricism to identify the ecological knowledge necessary to understand how nature works in relation to human interferences; that is, to find sustainable development. And science is the panacea to social improvement identifying the correct pathways for modernizing what schools do. For example, how social life can be changed to have a more progressive society (the long-range tasks for making the effective teacher and instructional improvement), and to create social justice and equality. The mantra of science gives legitimacy to the purpose of benchmarks, using "scientific evidence" to prove what reforms work, and identifying the authentic teacher who enacts the good intentions of society in the practices of school.

Second, education in ecology and sustainable development are never purely about nature, the physical world in the interaction with social practices and people. The formation of the curriculum is produced through different intersecting historical events. At one layer is the universalizing of the assumptions about the nature of phenomena as well as epistemic machinery practices of the different sciences. The pedagogical theories of the Americans Edward L. Thorndike and John Dewey, although different, express universalized notions of science and scientific method to explore how the child's mind should work and engage in solving problems. Thus, while the content varies in teaching physics, biology, astronomy, and zoology, for example, it is organized through a logic related to a generalized philosophy of science about rational thought. This notion of rational thought pervades, in different ways, and is then interpreted through organization criteria related to the teaching and psychologies of learning and childhood. What appears on the surface is a knowledge related to schooling but not the product of any systematic attempts to understand the social and cultural practices of the sciences in the production of knowledge.

This brings back an important element of Ideland's book. The notion of the rational and empirical in educating the child is not about some pure thought or transcendental rationality that is "science." The notions of rationality are linked to cultural principles about collective belonging and home through which the content of scientific concepts and principles are translated into theories of the child, pedagogy, and learning. This is perhaps a way to think about today's policy, media, and research on schooling in which science becomes a form of literacy, asking "Are children becoming scientifically literate and technologically knowledgeable so as to act as responsible citizens?" The curriculum and psychologies of learning are to effect the sensitivities, dispositions, and awarenesses that reach into the soul of the child; what Ideland discusses as affects, emotions and desires.

The focus on environmental education and sustainable development captures the dual sense of science. Science is the content for achieving the social good; that is, sustainable development is a redemptive discourse about how a more enlightened understanding of the relation of nature and humankind can be achieved. This knowledge is to overcome the negative effects of science and its misuse. But science entails the criteria for the particular selection and organization to "fit" into the curriculum. It is pedagogical principles about how children are to know, assess, interact, and effect change that intersects with the content taken from disciplinary practices of science. The pedagogical methods to elicit rationalities for problem-solving in the curriculum articulate a universalized notion of science as a way of how human mind should work and as the practice of ordering the decisions of everyday life.

Going against the grain. Ideland's book carefully intervenes in the orthodoxies through which the salvation and redemption themes of science are given concrete principles in organizing schooling and making kinds of people. The utopic aspirations are never merely about enacting hopes and dreams. They entail complex and historically concrete assemblages of ideas, concepts, and principles that form the political of schooling.

The notion of the political is about power that operates less through brute force and sovereign power but more as the subjectification or the productive quality of power. The latter is about the principles in ordering what is done, thought, and acted on in the productive process of life itself. I use political in the senses of Foucault's *governmentality* (1979), Rancière's (2006) *partition of the sensible,* and, if I can add, "sensibilities" to focus on affect. The notion of the political is what Deleuze and Guattari (1991/1994) argue about power (and the political): it is "not the sources, essences, and mechanisms of power; instead, the very structures seen as the origins of power presuppose its relations and are content to 'fix' them, as part of a function that is not productive but reproductive. There is no State, only state control, and the same holds for all other cases" (Deleuze & Guattari, 1991/1994, p. 75).

Ideland's study does not forego the more conventional notions of power that operate through social structures. The study's primary task, however, is to ask about the concrete rules and standards of the reason that order and classify environmental education; and how that reason has a materiality in producing differences in effort to exclude and abject in the name of good intentions. Ideland's book carefully travels through the landscape of Sweden programs and international reports for sustainable development and ecological education. She asks about the principles generated about the types of objects recognized, the classifications giving directions to explanations, the problems and evidence necessary for managing and predicting, and about the modalities on which change is calculated and administered. The principles that emerge have less to do with sustainable development, science, and ecology. Rather, they have more to do with creating collective belonging through individualization. That individualization paradoxically produces comparative cultural principles about different populations that the normalization and pathologization of the populations have little to do with science, per se.

While it would be easy to say at this point, "Why Sweden?" One might say: isn't Sweden of interest only to those in comparative education? The answer is clearly stated in this book. Sweden is not the case but the exemplar to explore the political phenomena of schooling. The theoretical approach and methodological considerations, as Ideland continually richly defines, raise issues about the exclusion and abjections in efforts of inclusion through pedagogical projects. These epistemic principles that order the events of Swedish schooling circulate with different historical nuances and complexities in multiple historical spaces and with the political of modernity and schooling.

The Swedish study makes possible understanding how cultural principles of national exceptionalism leach into how school programs are narrated and images of difference produced. This notion of national exceptionalism is not unique to Sweden but takes on particular historical principles about the relation of people and collective norms that include affects in cognitive forms. Sweden has positioned itself since the middle of the twentieth century as the international moral guardian to which people around the world. It appears as the exemplar of the caring and welfare state that serves as the model of progressive concerns about humanity. This is precisely the point that Ideland seeks to explore as an issue of power and the political of schooling. Sweden is an exemplar of the case to explore the political of modern schooling that is not provincialized by the boundaries of the nation. The exceptionalism of Sweden produces a continuum of values that differentiations the self and others.

Four themes underlined about the politics of knowledge in the practices and study of schooling stand out for the study of schooling.

First, *The Eco-Certified Child* poses an important challenge to the common sense of schooling, policy, and studies of education. It asks, "What kinds of people are being made through the practices of schooling?" Of course, the language of schooling and its research is the noble enterprise of social improvement and learning, not about changing people. In fact, the major strands of research articulate the logic of good intentions that if the right mixture of policies, science, and effective teaching is obtained, schooling will produce individual happiness and progress to society (*as well as furthering national projects*). The social intent of schooling and research is to actualize good intentions through producing the profession and authentic teacher. To paraphrase contemporary research on teacher education, the active, participatory and collaborative child will make reasonable decisions that respect nature for the good of all humankind. The eco-certified child will have certitude of inclusion where "all" children can reach their potential and have voice.

Yet stripped of the moral entitlements, the approved certified child and education for sustainable development is about a particular kind of person. That person is not merely about what knowledge is cognitively known. The attention is directed to the interior of the child in the production of subjectivities with affective and emotional qualities. Ideland documents how particular characteristics of the child, who is "the good" and possesses characteristics of self-confidence, willingness to change and engagement, linked to particular notions of collective belonging and "home." That collective belonging embodies a particular Swedish Exceptionalism about the nation and its people. The self-confident child, for example, is one that romanticizes nature as part of its aesthetics of being bodily and culturally Swedish! To be ecologically aware is to see one's self as the incarnation of the land with the landscape having uniqueness and aesthetics for others to admire, understand and emulate as the mode of life that makes a sustainable world. The national images of an ecological phantasm are universalized as the land where people live with bicycles, wind turbines, and fields of grain that play on the politics of emotions. While the phantasm is projected, Ideland continually checks the material realities of the sustainability of the image in the governing of the child.

Second, the good intentions of science education are built on the assumption that there is truth in the labeling. In fact, the teaching of environmental education is for children's learning about science to obtain thoughtful and rational interactions between humans and the physical and natural world. The school curriculum and research that focus on its reforms are clear-cut in expressing this assumption: how science education in programs can produce the appreciation and the knowledge necessary for a sustainable world. This assumption about what is named as environmental education and sustainable development is so ingrained in the contemporary mindset that it converts the task of research and teaching into finding the effective pedagogical knowledge about children's learning so that they can contribute positively to the world. Ah, if only schools can make all children rational, all people and the world will then become reasonable as a consequence!

But now, it should be clear that the problem in the study of sustainable development education is not about learning science. Ideland's study makes clear that there is little truth in the labeling! The enactments of the good intentions are nothing but illusions that, however, have real implications and effects. *The Eco-Certified Child* makes obvious that the premise that what is named as school subjects is not what is taught. The analysis offers a broad and sustained examination of different social spaces to explore how the certification of the ecologically conscious child appears historically having little to do with the science as historical fields in the production of knowledge. What is taken as science are the concepts, generalizations, and propositions of the sciences that are assembled and connected in the organizing of the social and cultural spaces of schooling. Moving disciplinary practices into the school is a creative act that does not just reproduce that original knowledge. Science in the curriculum becomes the translation of the knowledge-content of sciences into organizational theories of instruction and psychologies designed to administer children's learning. The pedagogical practices embody cultural theses that connects individuality to principles of collective belonging and "home." Ideland calls these kinds of people generated in schooling as "the free-range" and "eco-certified" child that is shaped through social and cultural values that do not relate back to the practices of the sciences.

The translation of disciplinary knowledge into what is taught in schools is like an alchemy, analogous to the Medieval alchemies that were magically to turn base metals into pure gold (Popkewitz, 2004). Like the alchemists, the curriculum entails moving disciplinary fields designed for the production of knowledge into the spaces of schooling.

The translation and transportation practices are magical transformation and transmogrifications designed through principles of pedagogical knowledge, including psychologies of the child, the architectural organization of schools, and the administrative categories and time dimensions of classroom practices. These alchemic practices of schooling are designed to produce particular kinds of people, not the scientist, but the citizen, for example. The making of the eco-certified child makes visible that the particular epistemic, social and institutional spaces have much to do with cultural theses about who the child is and should be, but not about science. Education in sustainable development is about who children are and should be.

This returns again to the case of the book that uses science in civic processes of education, yet its trajectory of analysis is more profound. The book is an exploration of the broader issues of schooling and the political in shaping and fashioning what is said, thought and acted on. The movements and translations of the alchemy of the curriculum have a historicity and mutability as they are assembled and connected. It is this historicity and mutability that enables the connection of sustainable development education in Sweden to international agencies and programs in which the case is not geographical but epistemic and about the political.

Third, and again, tied to the previous, the making of the eco-certified child is not about who the child is but about actualizing desires about potentialities of society and children-to-be. This notion of desire and potentiality is not personal and psychological, but historical assemblages in the Deleuzian sense of actualizing the experiences of the present as universalized potentialities of what is to become (Delueze, 1968/1994; Delueze & Parnet, 1987). This inscription of desire is so commonsensical that it is overlooked in contemporary human sciences. It seems almost commonsensical and "reasonable" to insert potentialities as the object of schooling: "Do school fulfill their obligations for preparing children to rationally plan for their future happiness in work, social affairs and as citizen? How can instruction be improved to enable children to have a lifetime as lifelong learners? Desires are embedded in international assessments that usher in the promise that all nations and schools can live what is historically specific as the universal transcendental promise about human potentialities. OECD's Programme for International Student Assessment (PISA) (http://www.oecd.org/pisa) of school systems in over 72 countries measures and differentiates schools as preparing for children's "well-being" and competencies to participate in the future.

If one looks carefully at the notion of change that pervades the social, anthropological, and psychological sciences, one will find that human sciences are not about the present, but about changing the present to a desired future. That future is embedded in the categories of the theories and methods of science that contain a priori assumptions about a desired world about what was hoped for.

Ideland's analysis makes visible this governing of the present as about desires. Those desires are oriented to principles about the potentialities of what society and people should be. Sustainable development is about change and the future; both directed to actualizing particular cultural theses about who people should be. Its project is utopic, but, of course, the utopic qualities are not spoken as such. They are embedded in how things are ordered in a manner that orients thoughts and actions. These desires are sometimes expressed conceptually as socialization, acculturation, learning, equity of learning outcomes, and the professional teacher who works for social improvement—all these activities are directed to what one should be and not only about what one is. In this study, the potentialities are in how numbers are used to talk about Sweden as the nation who heroically faces environmental concerns that elide its economic footprints to project images that have the importance of international moral claims about the nation's identity and its modes of living in relation to others.

The fourth theme is the comparative reasoning about kinds of people. Sustainable development and the ecological minded child are not only about desires to be actualized as the good society and a good child. It is also about shame and guilt, and about exclusions in efforts to create an inclusive society (and the world as seen from its particular historical place). This comparativeness is not straightforward. It is expressed in the cultural distinctions about the classification of the eco-certified child as cosmopolitan kinds of person whose human agency produces the sustainable environment. The characteristics of the good child generate also principles about who is not that child (and society). It is the child who does not participate, not appreciate the ways in which the Swedish child practices environmental awareness, and not live within a highly technological and energy consuming society, within which sustainability obtains its drive. The Other is the person who has resignation, cultural passivity, spontaneity, and non-reflectiveness. It is *the affect aliens*, students who do not see the point of changing their habits, not feel the right thing, and not act for the right reason. The Others are placed is spaces abjected; positioned as outside of the European modes of expressing consumption, commitments and who embody the dangers to the utopic visions instantiated in the curriculum. The populations are discussed as South African Blacks and Chinese who need to "learn," emulate, and express the Swedish (Northern) superiorities as the norms if they are ever going to be modern.

That comparativeness is embodied in the inscriptions of belonging, exclusion, and abjection embedded in the reasoning that is instantiated in the education for sustainable development. The inscriptions of representations and identities of students and teachers are given as universal qualities of potentialities from which, as Deleuze (1968/1994) argues, differences are established. The representations are objectifications that appear as principles about "all children" learn. The "all" functions as a unity in which a continuum of value is produced from the universalized representations and identities. The potentialities-to-be simultaneously engender principles about what is without those potentialities, abjected as outside of its livable spaces. What does not fit is, then, placed and ironically experienced as insensible, unrecognizable, and not "civilized." The names for the civilized are now psychologicalized and personalized as the child "lacking" motivation and self-esteem.

The universal performs as double gestures: the hope of making kinds of children who participate in society simultaneously embodies fears about the dangers and dangerous populations who do not fit into the spaces of belonging. The potentialities-not-to-be is the child in Sweden who acts for the wrong reasons, and does not appreciate the affect of the pastoral beauty of nature in constructing a desirable living, among others. The internal and external "Others" violate the narratives and images of the child as pure and untouched but responsible for the future.

These four themes play out in the text with a beauty of language and a playfulness of ideas that are elegant. That elegance is accompanied not only with the depth and nuance of argument, but also with the naming of phenomena. There are the *free-range child*, the *eco-certified emotions*, *eco-certified bodies*, and *unchildish children*. It is my mouth watering with the reference to Ben & Jerry Ice Cream only to recognize that the affect entails commodifications of complex relations and the effects of power. The language gets at the heart of the making of differences through talking about the utopic as what is *natural with no artificial additives*.

The playfulness of naming is part of the seriousness of the task undertaken. This naming of the study is what Ideland calls a multisite desk study; an ethnography of books and policy documents. The ethnography is to treat the archive as what is produced by the culture of schooling and as what has a materiality whose statements are examined to understand how intelligibility is given the schooling. It is to read the visual culture in ways of how numbers become *centers of calculation* and how charts govern the boundaries of what are seemingly rational and logical choices. Ideland gives visibility to how these centers of calculation embody the mechanism in which programs of government are articulated and made operable through depoliticizing the political by making them appear as objective. In this manner, the multisite desk study provides a way to understand the materialities of knowledge book, the limits of dichotomies of nominalism (ideas) as different from the real, and the tendency to dismiss discourses in documents as different from what "teachers really do and say."

Finally, and to the problem of a science of education and the problem of change, the book brings to the surface the significance of critique as a strategy of change and of rethinking "method" and "the empirical" in research. Its engagement with the social commitments and good intentions of school are evident through the very choice of examining the political of schooling and in the concepts that direct attention to the paradoxes of schooling in the production of the self, difference, and otherness.

The engagement in critique is a form of optimism in what Blumenburg (1966/1983), a German social historian, talked about "renunciation," and what Lynn Fendler, a colleague at Michigan State University, calls "whistle-blowing." It is to continually ask about how we have arrived at the present and its limits as a method of thinking about change. *This second sense of critique* is to account for the rules and standards that order the present in order to make possible alternatives other than what are already taken as natural. Change, in this strategy of research, is embodied in the *opening up of spaces, beyond what exists as its ordering of "things."* The unthinking that the book compels us to engage in is a practice of the possibilities of change.

Again, Ideland's arguments go against the grain, and are central for understanding contemporary education, its social commitments and the political of modernity.

Madison, USA   Thomas S. Popkewitz
August 2018   University of Wisconsin-Madison

References

Blumenburg, H. (1966/1983). *The legitimacy of the modern age* (R. Wallace, Trans.). Cambridge: MIT Press.

Deleuze, G. (1968/1994). *Difference and repetition* (P. Patton, Trans.). New York: Athlone Press of Columbia University.

Deleuze, G., & Parnet, C. (1977/1987). *Dialogues* (H. Tomlinson & B. Habberjam, Trans.). New York: Columbia University Press.

Foucault, M. (1979). Governmentality. *Ideology and Consciousness, 6*, 5–22.

Nye, D. E. (1999). *American technological sublime.* Cambridge, MA: MIT Press.

Popkewitz, T. S. (2004). The alchemy of the mathematics curriculum: Inscriptions and fabrications of the child. *American Educational Journal, 41*(4), 3–34.

Popkewitz, T. S. (Ed.). (2005). *Inventing the modern self and John Dewey: Modernities and the traveling of pragmatism in education.* New York: Palgrave Macmillan Press.

Popkewitz, T. S., Khurshid, A., & Zhao, W. (2014). Comparative studies and the reasons of reason: Historicizing differences and "seeing" reforms in multiple modernities. In L. Vega (Ed.), *Empires, post-coloniality, and interculturality. New challenges for comparative education* (pp. 21–43). Rotterdam: Sense.

Rancière, J. (2006). *The politics of aesthetics*. New York: Bloomsbury Academic.

Series Introduction

Our primary goal for the *Palgrave Studies in Education and the Environment* series is to showcase new developments and advances in the scholarship of education and environment.

A key dimension of this aim is to promote theoretically-rich work through contributions that include empirical and conceptual studies progressing critical analysis and practice in environmental education and related fields. In other words, as with our publishers, we expect the series to realise two outcomes: (i) advance the theoretical depth and sophistication of scholarship on education and environment, and (ii) offer critical orientations to such matters of public concern.

Why have we developed such expectations for this series?

First, there is our experience and sense of the strengths and weaknesses of existing scholarship in this area, echoed in the comments of our colleagues, mentors, and students. These raise a critical question for us: whether some of the underlying orientations of current and prevailing ways of conceptualising and enacting environmental and sustainability education are *fundamentally limited* and *need shaking up*. This impetus pertains to both outcomes identified above, in that there is scope for broader and deeper theoretical engagement, as well as further consideration of the real implications of the scholarship for education and the environment. The series thus aims to highlight and support critical and theoretical scholarship that matters for how we live and educate in the world.

Second, to address such concerns, the series should enable readers to engage interdisciplinary and diverse perspectives on education and environment, particularly as these relate to domains of policy, practice, and research. Thus, we expect studies in this series to span a range of traditions, scales, and approaches, from the micro level of empirical thick description to the meta-level of conceptual analysis and synthesis. Critically engaging with contemporary topics and issues demands high-quality contributions that also both tap into a growing body of theoretical scholarship relevant to education and environment, and innovate in this space.

The series thus provides established and new scholars with both a venue and an avenue for examining the interdisciplinary intersections of environment and education; challenging the theorizations and enactment of environment and sustainability-related education through critical, creative, and compelling scholarship.

We hope you enjoy engaging with the study that follows, and find it a fitting contribution to the series.

Melbourne, Australia   Alan Reid
Saskatoon, Canada   Marcia McKenzie

Preface

This book problematizes the good intentions of Environmental and Sustainability Education (ESE). It questions how school makes up standards for who lives the environmentally friendly life and the opposite. Who is constructed as a threat to the world and by what means? Is the common understanding of the sustainable life really sustainable, or has environmental engagement been reduced into treasured identity for a white, educated and economically strong middle class? How can we teach for sustainability without being politically and culturally trapped in positions of superiority and subordination; understandings of who is included respectively excluded from the category of good citizens? The ultimate aim of the book is to discuss what comes along, unintentionally, with the good intentions to educate for a sustainable society.

This means that the book is critically approaching a field which is both important and with the best of intentions—namely to deal with the enormous challenges such as environmental disasters and social injustices. Even though I deconstruct and criticize the practice of ESE I need to emphasize that the world suffers from severe environmental problems, caused by humans and affecting humans, animals and the ecological system. In times of alternative facts and political systems that work *against* the environment, it might thus seem odd—maybe even dangerous—to criticize a practice aiming to work *for* the environment. However, my aim is just the opposite, I would like to illuminate how good intentions *also* can be impregnated by injustices and inequalities in order to think of new ways of approaching the problems.

The deconstruction of this treasured practice, ESE, is made through analyzing cultural characteristics of what I call the eco-certified child. This is a playing with words; what if there were standards for environmentally humans, just as there is a protocol for what food that can be certified as organic? What would that protocol include, and would it really be good for the ecological system? Important to say is that the notion the eco-certified child does not refer to a real child by flesh and blood. Rather, it should be understood as a discursive figuration of the child which is organizing our understanding of how to be and act to be able to pass as an environmentally friendly person in our time. In that sense the eco-certified child is neither a fiction nor a real person, but something in-between—a discursive figuration that conditions how different categories of people actually can live and a deconstruction of the taken for granted can make us think new thoughts.

The word child is used with a reference to Thomas S. Popkewitz work on the cosmopolitan child, a cultural thesis that is organizing how we can think of education in general. However, child is here not referring to a specific age, it is used to think of the unfinished citizen—the one that is seen as in the making and still possible to shape through education. We all (even adults) can be that child, subjected to a general will to shape a certain kind of society through fostering, information and education. An analysis of educational practices says a lot of this societal will, which needs to be constantly questioned in order to see what the effects of the politics are and can possibly be.

Malmö, Sweden   Malin Ideland

Acknowledgements

This book would never have been written or published without help from friends, family, and colleagues. Thanks to Per Hillbur and Claes Malmberg, my research companions in the project "The eco-certified child." Thanks to my colleagues at the Faculty Education and Society for intellectual conversations, critical comments, new perspectives, encouragement, and friendship. I owe special thanks to Anna Jobér, Margareta Serder, Helen Hasslöf, Mats Lundström, Susanna Hedenborg, Catarina Christiansson, Gudrun Jonsdottir, Nils Ekelund, Camilla Safrankova, Christian Rydberg, Anna Wirstedt, Magdalena Sjöstrand-Öhrfelt, Therese Lindgren, and Laurence Delacour. Thanks to colleagues at the universities in Örebro, Uppsala, Stockholm, Madison-Wisconsin, Vienna, Kristianstad, Stockholm, and Linköping, especially to Maria Andrée, Tora Holmberg, Tom Popkewitz, Daniel Tröhler, and Paola Valero for friendship, hospitality, and intellectual engagement. Maria Andrée, Lena Hansson, Tora Holmberg, Per Hillbur, Claes Malmberg, Margareta Serder, and Daniel Tröhler have also been co-authors of different articles function as an important base for the book.

Thanks to Henrik Celander and Lena Andersson who published the Swedish edition of the book, *Den KRAV-märkta människan*, and who also happily let me publish an English version at Palgrave Macmillan. Thanks to Alan Crozier for translating parts of the manuscript and to Rebecca Wyde and Eleanor Christie at Palgrave Macmillan who provided exceptional guidance throughout the process. Not at least, thank you Marcia McKenzie and Alan Reid for encouragement to write the book.

The Swedish Research Council funded the research project (DNR 2011-5907). Faculty of Education and Society at Malmö University supported the translation into English.

At last my family, Jens, Tova, Malva… what would my world be without you?

Malin Ideland

Contents

Abbreviations

EE	Environmental Education
ESD	Education for Sustainable Development
ESE	Environmental and Sustainability Education
GAP	Global Action Plan
GERM	Global Education Reform Movement
GHA	Global Hectare
MUVIN	Miljöundervisning i Norden (Environmental Education in the Nordic Countries)
OECD	Organisation for Economic Co-operation and Development
OMEP	Organisation Mondiale pour l'Éducation Préscolaire
PISA	Programme for International Student Assessment
SD	Sustainable Development
UN	United Nations
UNEP	United Nations Environment Programme
UNESCO	United Nations Educational, Scientific and Cultural Organization
WWF	World Wildlife Fund for Nature

1

Making the Other Through Good Intentions

Abstract This chapter is an introduction to the book, describing the aim, empirical data and theoretical framework. Since the book seeks to problematize the incontestability of Environmental and Sustainability Education (ESE) and how to be an environmentally friendly student (the eco-certified child), it departs from Foucault's thoughts on how discourses organize how it is possible to live in a certain context and how "kinds of" desirable and undesirable people are made inside these discourses. Ultimately the book aims to shed light on what is "into the bargain" with good intentions to create a sustainable society; how the idea of a common future in fact makes distinctions between social classes, races, and nationalities. The chapter outlines how these analyses are done from theories deconstructing normality and the Other.

Keywords Environmental and Sustainability Education · Foucault The Other

Mmmm, cotton candy. Yummy. Maybe not as tasty as Fairly Nuts or Vermonster, but very good. I am in the "taste room" at Ben & Jerry's ice cream factory in Vermont, USA. It is the last stop (before the obligatory souvenir shop), and the peak of the guided tour of the factory. The ice cream tastes amazingly good, and even better when I take a closer look at the walls of the room. On them hang paintings and posters with the company's slogan: Peace, Love and Ice Cream. I read: "We strive to minimize our negative impact on the environment, from cow to cone" and "We seek to support nonviolent ways to achieve peace & justice." It is not only the ice cream that is good—maybe one can become good through eating it? Through something so simple as a conscious choice of ice cream, it seems possible to contribute to saving our threatened environment and to fight against social injustices. Good that we went by plane from Sweden to the USA, drove to Vermont and experienced this!

Ben & Jerry's is in many ways an exemplary company. Their tasty ice creams are not just organically produced and fair-trade certified. Besides the fact that the company has been involved in a number of social justice projects, in the home state of Vermont as well as in other places in the world. During 2015 they launched the ice cream cone Save our Swirled with the aim of highlighting climate change. While finishing the writing of this book, they engaged in the Swedish and EU political debate about refugees and for more generous rules for asylum. Their trademark is a symbol of the possibility of humane and sustainable business (Edmondson, 2014).

Certainly, the world needs more companies like this. But one can also understand Ben & Jerry's as a symbol of how the solution to complex sustainability and environment issues has been culturally translated into individual consumption choices. Laws seem out of fashion; instead it is up to you and me to become knowledgeable about problems and solutions and to make sustainable choices, like buying sustainable ice cream. Michel Foucault (1980) wrote that we need to understand power in this kind of society as if the king's head has been cut off. Governing and exercise of power does not just happen through state government, but through people's souls and their will to feel and appear normal. As will be discussed later, this means that the individual's intentions, actions and feelings become entangled with global environmental problems.

Back to the ice cream. The website YouthXChange, which is supported by the United Nations organizations UNESCO and UNEP as well as business corporations, suggests a number of ways for youngsters to contribute to a better world. One suggestion is to buy Ben & Jerry's ice cream under the heading: Ice Cream with a Mission:

> The company has a progressive, non-partisan social mission that seeks to meet human needs and eliminate injustices in local, national and international communities by integrating these concerns into their day-to-day business activities. The company's focus is on children and families, the environment and sustainable agriculture on family farms. (http://www.youthxchange.net)

In my home country Sweden a 0.5 liter can of this ice cream costs around 60 kronor, which means around 7 US dollars. In other words: the United Nations, as a symbol and an organization, is used to promote an ice cream brand which is as tasty as it is expensive. How can that be possible? To be able to understand this one needs to understand the context. The platform YouthXChange is a part of a global educational reform. In 2014 the United Nations' decade of Education for Sustainable Development (ESD) 2005–2014 came to an end (https://en.unesco.org/themes/education-sustainable-development/what-is-esd/un-decade-of-esd). After that the Global Action Plan (GAP) was initiated (http://www.globalactionplan.com). This pedagogical discourse and practice, which today mostly is referred to either as Education for Sustainable Development (ESD) or as Environmental and Sustainability Education (ESE) has its roots in environmental education (EE) in the 1960s and 1970s.[1] During the early nineties, the environmental debate was widened and put into a context of social and economic factors. The notion of sustainable development became a symbol of our time. In *Our Common Future*, also known as the Brundtland Report, sustainable development was described as follows: "Sustainable development is development that meets the needs of the present without compromising the ability of future generations to meet their own needs" (UN, 1987). To put it briefly, it is a matter of using the earth's resources responsibly, and striving for a more equal society. Social and economic development for "everyone"—with ecological sustainability—is an important goal.

---

[1] For a history of EE, ESD, and ESE see e.g. Gough (2006), Palmer (1998).

There is criticism both against the development paradigm and against the way that social and economic factors are assessed as ecological, particularly in the research field of education for sustainability (e.g. Jickling & Wals, 2008; Kopnina, 2012). As a result, people talk of ESE rather than ESD, stressing Education and Environment rather than Development. This brings in the broad sustainability perspective, while simultaneously emphasizing the ecological problems and toning down the development discourse. In this book, I will use the term ESE for the same reason.

Education has been held up as an important tool for achieving a sustainable society. The idea was—and still is—that everybody can help, that the world can be saved with the aid of education, engagement, and a will to do the right thing. Children and adolescents—and also adults—should therefore be educated and socialized in new lifestyles, demanding ecological, economic, and social sustainability. What this means in purely concrete terms is harder to define. As pointed out by several scholars (e.g. Bengtsson & Östman, 2013; González-Gaudiano, 2005; Gough & Scott, 2006; Hillbur, Ideland, & Malmberg, 2016), ESD, and ESE are "slippery" concepts. This makes them receptive to political and societal changes. They can be given meaning depending on how, when, and where they are used and work as "an airport hub for meaning making" (Mannion, Biesta, Priestley, & Ross, 2011, p. 444). This is clear in the way that "sustainability" is used by companies in their codes of behavior or in justifications of political decisions, in applications for research funding, or in selling products. Sustainability is not merely a political will; it is also a symbol which means that the United Nations can be used to advertise a brand of ice cream in an educational context, under the cover of saving the world. Sustainable development cannot be contested. Who could be against working for sustainability?

This book aims to problematize the incontestability of sustainable development and the notion of being an environmentally friendly person in general, and a pupil in particular. I want to discuss from a critical standpoint how the talk of sustainable development and environmental consciousness—in school and in society—construct and maintain a cultural theses for the desirable child; the eco-certified child. I also wish to problematize how this construction of the normal, desirable child simultaneously single out individuals and groups as problems—as the dangerous population. Does the understanding of the dangerous population really have anything to do with the effects of lifestyles on the environment? Or is it a matter of other social categories, for example, to do with class, race, and nationality? Ultimately the book aims to shed light on what we get "into the bargain" with our good intentions to create a sustainable society. How can we understand that the idea of a shared world and a common future actually serves to make distinctions—between people, age groups, social classes, races, and nationalities?

The book is an outcome of a research project at Malmö University, funded by the Swedish Research Council: "The Eco-certified Child: On Subject Constructions in Education for Sustainable Development."[2] The project explored cultural understandings of what environmentally friendly people are supposed to be like, in teaching material and policy texts aimed at school and preschool, and how the image of what was named "the eco-certified child" simultaneously (re)produces class-specific, racial and national norms. Distinctions are made—unintentionally—between people. Another aim of the project was to problematize the role assigned to children in the work for sustainability. What does it mean that children are made responsible for the future of the world? Through illuminating and problematizing the good intentions of a culturally and pedagogically elevated practice (ESE), unintended inclusions and exclusions into the categories of normal and deviant human beings can be disrupted.

Think We Must

This book is an attempt to critically approach a field which is important and which has the best of intentions, namely, to deal with enormous challenges such as environmental disasters and social injustices.

---

[2]Swedish title: "Det KRAV-märkta barnet: Om subjektskonstruktioner i lärande för hållbar utveckling." The research project was financed by the Swedish Research Council 2012–2015, reg. no. 2011-5907. PI was Malin Ideland, co-researchers were Per Hillbur and Claes Malmberg.

The problems are real, no doubt of that. I don't underestimate either the explanations or all the consequences for humans, animals, and the ecological system. On the contrary, this is one of the most important challenges for the world. Despite that, or rather because of that, I seek to problematize environmental actions as well as children's play, emotions, and knowledge. Below I will claim that practices aiming to make children and youngsters happy can be problematic, as well as the attempt of including "everyone" in the sustainability project. I will also suggest that helping can be seen as a colonial practice and that tolerance is an exercise of power. Through these disruptions of the commonsensical good, I emphasize that it can simultaneously be impregnated by injustices and inequalities. In this process I take on the role of what Sarah Ahmed (2010) calls (feminist) killjoy—to problematize the good intention and recognize that it may have problematic consequences that might even prevent real change.

In a TED talk, with over 15 million views, the author Chimamanda Ngozi Adichie (2009) brings up the problem of "the single story": that one strong narrative about a category of people, a country, a continent becomes an established truth. For instance, Adichie shares an anecdote from her own childhood. She, a black girl born and raised in Nigeria, wrote children's books about white children, longing for the snow and drinking ginger beer. This was the single story about "children in books." Similarly, there is one single story about Africa as poor, corrupt, and plagued by war and starvation. Adichie states that even if this narrative about Africa is not false, it isn't the only possible one. There are so many different stories that can be told—about Africa, but also about education, environment, and sustainability. Taking on the challenge, this book adopts a critical stance in order to problematize the single story, how it has become a hegemonic truth and how it has (most likely) unintended consequences.

The beautiful rhetoric and pictures characterizing the discourse of ESE and environmental engagement obscure injustices produced through the very good intentions. Naomi Klein writes aptly that we are politically and culturally trapped in our imagination of environmental issues and social injustices; we need to challenge the ways we see and talk about them. At the end of the day it comes down to what Donna Haraway (2016) writes about in her book with the mind-teasing title *Staying with the Trouble:* "Think we must; we must think. Actually think, not like Eichmann the Thoughtless" (p. 47). The Eichmann referred to is the Nazi war criminal Adolf Eichmann, whose unwillingness or inability to think for himself, instead referring to a bureaucratic system, is Hanna Arendt's famous example of the banality of evil (Arendt, 1963). The evil lay in the commonplace thoughtlessness, not in the lack of knowledge of what was happening (Haraway, 2016, pp. 36ff.). Think we must; we must think.

Being in the Truth

To be able to think outside the hegemonic truth, theoretical tools are needed. In the upcoming sections I will introduce the ones I have been inspired by and learned from in my analyses of the ESE discourse. Throughout its rather short history, ESE has (roughly speaking from at least a Swedish perspective) changed from being a practice based on explicit characteristics for environmentally friendly ways of living in the 1970s, to today's emphasis on a pluralistic approach which aims to make room for different subjectivities (Öhman, 2006). The desirable child constructed by the current discourse of ESE is the modern, cosmopolitan child—the reasonable and empathetic problem solver who listens to different opinions before taking a stand and acting. But ESE holds an inherent conflict; it aims to promote a pluralistic, democratic approach at the same time as it has an important and urgent problem to solve.[3] This means that the child (like any human being), through its "free will," is supposed to voluntarily adapt to a certain way of thinking and living at the same time as a pluralistic discourse characterizes the practice. It is an illustrative example of Foucault's (e.g. 1980, 1983) theories of power: how to make the individual will comply with the common will without any external force. In this theoretical section, I will elaborate on my understanding of how governing—not beyond, but through—free will is possible (Ideland, 2017).

---

[3]There is criticism against the pluralistic approach, precisely because the issue of environmental degradation and the problems of other species are excluded from the discussion when individual opinion, rather than the effect, is important (Kopnina, 2012; Kopnina & Cherniak, 2016).

The eco-certified child, a concept that I play with in this book, is not a real person of flesh and blood. It is rather a kind of figuration that is historically and culturally constructed, functioning as a cultural proto-col for how children are supposed to act, the demands that must be sat-isfied (Castañeda, 2002). In other words, it is a stereotyped ideal image of the environmentally friendly person, in the shape of a child. "Child" here does not refer to a specific age but is a metaphor for the notion of a malleable—unfinished—person. "What is the child but a human in an incomplete form, which must acquire the necessary traits and skills to live as an adult?" as Claudia Castañeda asks (2002, p. 1). She continues by arguing that embedded in the assumptions of the child is "potential-ity rather than an actuality, a becoming rather than a being: an entity in the making" (ibid.). These assumptions make the child educatable, and also an investment for the future. A citizen in the making, comprising a promise of a better society (Popkewitz, 2012).

The eco-certified child is no innocent figure; it does something to us and our ideas about normality and deviation, about good and evil. By connecting different attributes to different bodies—genders, age groups, skin colors, geographical places—it "makes up" different kinds of peo-ple (Hacking, 2006), categories of people whose possibilities are con-ditional. Because the figuration is reconstructed time and again, it also makes a great many demands of people if they are to be perceived as citizens contributing to a sustainable world. Ian Hacking (1995) calls it "looping effects"; discursive constructions act on the world in highly concrete and material ways. The narratives not only describe the world and its inhabitants, they actually produce ways in which we *can* think, talk, act, and live (Foucault, 1991). The ways in which one can live dif-fer depending not only on material living conditions, but also on how you are categorized and positioned in society. This book seeks to take this discursive figuration to pieces and to discuss what makes it appear like an obvious truth, and what it does to our view of what you are sup-posed to be like if you want to be reckoned as environmentally friendly. This will be done by analyzing "governing technologies": rhetorical and visual devices that (re)produce the figuration in a way that we take for granted, making it "natural" and irrefutable (e.g. Foucault, Senellart, & Davidson, 2007; Rose & Miller, 2010). The governing technologies organize how we are supposed to act, but by illuminating them we can expose the commonsensical truth in a way that enables us to question what it does to us and the world and discuss alternative ways of talking about the environment, sustainability, and human beings.

As Foucault expresses it, being in a discourse, belonging there, and being regarded as "normal" means "being in the truth" (Foucault, 1971). The eco-certified child is materializing "the truth" as regards issues of environment and sustainability. By appealing to accepted ideas of reason and normality, the discourse (re)produces cultural understandings of who lives a good life and indicates those who need to change in order not to risk threatening the world with their lifestyle; those who become the Other. This is also how Foucault—with his concept of governmentality[4]—explains how people can be "steered," not in opposition to but *through* their "free will" (Foucault, 1991; Foucault et al., 2007; Hacking, 2006; Serder & Ideland, 2016). Foucault (1990, p. 86) writes: "power is tolerable only on condition that it mask a substantial part of itself. Its success is proportional to its ability to hide its own mechanisms." Steering people in our "advanced liberal society" is not done from the throne (laws and rules), but through the longing and willingness of citizens to fit into the picture of the normal and reasonable person (Rose & Miller, 2010). The more taken-for-granted (masked) the discourse is, the more effective it is. This steering—which is sometimes defined as neoliberal, at other times as advanced liberal—with a reluctance to regulate, has been made possible, among many other things, by the growing fear of a strong state in the postwar era (Hursh, Henderson, & Greenwood, 2015).[5] In this political ideology, a person can only be free when liberated from the state and able to make choices in a free market. But a person's free will must go in the same direction as the general will—which may seem like an inherent irony in the advanced liberal society. The freedom is therefore regulated, not least of all with

---

[4]There is a body of literature discussing green governmentality for the environmental area. I will not go into that, but may mention, e.g. Lloro-Bidart (2017), Luke (1999), Soneryd and Uggla (2015).

[5]Hursh et al. (2015) have conducted a broad (although, as they point out, too short) survey and analysis of neoliberalism in society and in environmental education. McKenzie, Bieler, and McNeil (2015) likewise provide an overview of the neoliberal turn in ESE.

reference to the security of the nation—or indeed the survival of the planet (cf. Rose & Miller, 2010). Free—responsible and informed— choices should be made in relation to the general will and the security of the population (Foucault et al., 2007).

The Making of the Other

This understanding of how people are governed means, to use Foucault's words, that power is not repressive and limiting but in fact productive. The discourse does something to us, it makes us talk and act in specific ways. And it makes us refrain from talking and acting in other ways. The discourse in Foucault's sense does not only consist of what is said, but also what is unsaid (Foucault, 1971). Or, as Rodney Carter (2006, p. 223), puts it: "There is no speech without silence, otherwise there would just be unmodulated cacophony; likewise there would be no silence without speech, just a universal meaningless, emptiness." Everything can't be said, but we need to scrutinize what stories are missing. What is left out is also a kind of storytelling, and by emphasizing some perspectives, events, and narratives, others are hidden, silent, or even unspeakable in a certain context (Billig, 1999; Kulick, 2005). It is often marginalized groups' stories that are not told, or told from the perspective of the superior. That means that besides scrutinizing what is said, silent narratives also will be considered as a kind of governing technologies organizing possible ways to write.

In this book I use the word (re)produce to describe what both the spoken and the unspoken discourses "do"; it is often accepted truths that are reproduced, while the figure of the eco-certified child actually produces something new. It does something to us that did not necessarily exist before. Among other things, the discourse has the effect that certain ways of life are reckoned as undesirable. In an environmental context this may perhaps seem self-evident: the problems in the environment have arisen as a result of human activities. But what is reckoned as undesirable is not always connected to the effect on the environment. Instead I will argue that the figure of the eco-certified child rather is effecting—(re)producing—distinctions between humans in terms of social class, nationality, and race. The discursive effect is something other than the expressed intention; the wish to point out the right way of living make up one part of the population as good citizens, other as dangerous; a threat to themselves as well as to the society in which they live (Nadesan, 2010). Thomas Popkewitz's book *Cosmopolitanism and the Age of School Reform: Science, Education, and Making Society by Making the Child* (2012) historicizes and problematizes the ideal cosmopolitan citizen of modernity. He shows how the American education system is based on this ideal, and how it has developed in history. But his study also points out that school reforms aimed at including all pupils in this ideal citizen also exclude by defining certain ways of life as problematic:

> Equally important, cosmopolitanism embodies a particular mode of organizing difference. That entails comparative installations that differentiate and divide those who are enlightened and civilized from those who do not have those qualities–the backward, the savage and the barbarian of the 19th century and the at-risk and delinquent child of the present. The universal and inclusive practices of school reforms that speak about inclusion locate difference and incomplete elements, points, and directions in the processes of inclusion and exclusion. (Popkewitz, 2012, p. 4)

The notion of the dangerous population is (re)produced through inclusive political initiatives such as "no child left behind." These unintentional effects Popkewitz conceptualizes as "double gestures of inclusion and exclusion." Total inclusion is a political illusion, and we must discuss what it means to try to include people *into something*, scrutinizing the inclusions and exclusions that are (re)produced through these good intentions. Moreover, the category of pupils who have to be included, those who deviate from the notion of the desirable students, often coincides with groups that are already stigmatized in society, such as immigrants, people with functional disabilities, those with low income or low grade of education (Popkewitz, 2012). Through the good intention to include everyone, or as in the case in this book, to save the world from environmental degradation, a polarization is made between Us, those who fit in, and the Other, those who are a problem. The Other functions as a counter to the normal, what We should not be. In this way, the Other is at once undesirable and indispensable. The Other threatens the order at the same time as s/he is indispensible for the understanding of the position in society as "normal," "environmentally friendly," "good" or "reasonable" (Butler, 1993; McClintock, 1995).

Wendy Brown (2006) has investigated and problematized how tolerance can be regarded as a way to create subordination and superordination, that is, to exercise power. Despite the good intentions of tolerance, it does something more, it "produces and positions subjects, orchestrates meanings and practices of identity, marks bodies and conditions political subjectivities" (Brown, 2006, p. 4). To tolerate someone or something is also to define what is normality and what is deviance—but it also means that one can become good by noticing and accepting this person or thing. Brown sees a problem in that "tolerance" normalizes and depoliticizes power relations by dressing them in a beautiful language of goodness and inclusion. The practice and the idea of tolerance—unintentionally—differentiate people. In exploring the good intention of sustainable development I am inspired in this book by Brown as regards how ESE—unintentionally?—(re)produces desirable subjects, marking out which bodies, behaviors, and feelings fit in or do not fit in, and hence dictates the conditions for people's ability to act politically.

The book explores how the Other is constructed in terms of class, nationality, and race. More refined theoretical tools for investigating this come from postcolonial theory, critical race theory, and whiteness studies. Postcolonial theory helps me to understand how ideas about the world that are based on colonial structures still organize the way we think and act. Stuart Hall (1992) writes that "the West" is done in relation to "the Rest" (see also Said, 1978). Hall shows how the Western world has used stereotypical "Others" to constitute and uphold a discourse of Western Enlightenment as, for example, rational and civilized compared to the Other as the dark side, forgotten, repressed, and denied. Gayatri Chakravorty Spivak (1988) conceptualizes it as epistemic violence; an exercise of power by limiting the understanding of valid knowledge. She sheds light on how notions of knowledge, civilization, and education have been used to undermine non-Western methods, or approaches to knowledge. By that, she problematizes not only the colonizers' use of science and technology, but also today's efforts to provide technology, medicine, and especially education to the "uncivilized" parts of the world. In these colonial processes the subaltern's voice is not heard. It is silenced through the epistemic violence of not recognizing him/her as "reasonable," "rational," or "scientific" (cf. Haraway, 2004, p. 88). Through modernity's connections between development, rationality, and the Western world (or the Global North), the governing technology of what Santiago Castro-Gómez (2002) calls coloniality. The concept of coloniality is offered as a way to escape the fact that the notion of postcolonialism presumes a "pre" and a "post." It is also a distinction in relation to colonialism, which refers to a specific historical period. Castro-Gómez writes: "…coloniality references a technology of power that persists today, founded on the 'knowledge of the other.' Coloniality is not modernity's 'past' but its 'other face'" (2002, p. 276). And in that sense, I study how it organizes how we consider ESE and the people that inhabit it—at home and in other places. It is a way of thinking of the world.

The book is also inspired by critical race studies and whiteness studies. For example, I use Sara Ahmed's (2010) critical race theories on how certain characteristics are attached to certain bodies—or certain kinds of people as Ian Hacking (1995) conceptualizes it. Ahmed takes the example of how "terrorism" is stuck to a man from the Middle East. Other examples are how "caring" sticks to a female body, of a certain age and with a certain look. Similarly, Gloria Ladson-Billings (1998) points out that in an American context, "intelligence," "science," and "middle-class-ness" are connected to whiteness, while "under-class," "welfare recipients," and "basketball players" become marginalized categories of blackness:

> The creation of these conceptual categories is not designed to reify a binary but rather to suggest how, in a racialized society where whiteness is positioned as normative, everyone is ranked and categorized in relation to these points of opposition. These categories fundamentally sculpt the extant terrain of possibilities even when other possibilities exist. (Ladson-Billings, 1998, p. 9)

Whiteness has for centuries been connected to desirable human qualities, such as rationality and beauty, building on an imperialistic historical narrative in which whiteness is represented as the "light of the world" (Dyer, 1993, 1997). Blackness, on the other hand, has represented the unknown, mystery, and danger. In other words, the attributes follow a traditional hierarchical cultural system—the governing technology of coloniality. Otherness can also be constructed through positive attributes, such as more natural or exotic. This cultural system structures what kinds of bodies have access to what spaces, as well as how different kinds of people can be acted upon (Ahmed, 2010; Essed, 1991; Puwar, 2004).

Reasonable Emotions

In recent years the research field of ESE has taken a keen interest in emotions, both the feelings that children and adolescents have about sustainability issues—often emotions of hopelessness and fear—and how these can be turned into positive feelings of optimism and empowerment. But there are also studies about the significance of emotions for learning, that as an individual one must be moved in order to be changed (e.g. Fröhlich, Sellmann, & Bogner, 2013; Håkansson, Östman, & Van Poeck, 2018; Kramming, 2017; Ojala, 2013; Otieno et al., 2014). In other words, emotions are viewed from the individual's perspective, as a psychological phenomenon, and closely linked to learning in the sense of change.

This book is also about emotions, not as something attached to the individual but how emotions are valued in society and thus contribute to the construction of normality and alterity. For this analysis I turn, again, to Sara Ahmed's work on the cultural politics of emotions. Emotions are often described as individual and even intimate, but Ahmed (among others) sees them as socially organizing the world. She aims to escape the psychological view of emotions as something that comes from the inside, entering the outside—the "inside out" perspective. Further, she distances her work from a group-psychology perspective, the outside entering the inside—the "outside in" perspective. Instead, she states that:

emotions create the very effect of the surfaces and boundaries that allow us to distinguish an inside and an outside in the first place. So emotions are not simply something "I" or "we" have. Rather it is through emotions, or how we respond to objects and others, that surfaces or boundaries are made: the "I" and the "we" are shaped by, and even take the shape of, contact with others. (Ahmed, 2014, p. 10)

Ahmed describes emotions as "sticky"; they glue communities together. But at the same time, emotions position the Other on the outside. This Other she calls the *affect alien*—the one who feels the "wrong" thing at the "right" time or the "right" thing at the "wrong" time (Ahmed, 2010). In other words, emotions are about attachments, about what connects us to such categories as "reasonable" or "empowered" and that which "holds us in place" (Ahmed, 2004, p. 27). Emotions do things on a cultural level: they set up the distinctions between normality and those who need to change to be included in that. Some emotions are elevated and seen as signs of cultivation and reason, while others are signs of the opposite—which could be either too strong or too weak feelings for a "reasonable" citizen.

In other words, emotions must be domesticated; the eco-certified child is reasonable. And education is a way to make the population reasonable so that they can tackle problems such as pollution. Daniel Tröhler (2009, 2011) talks of the educationalization of societal problems. Education is viewed as a way of solving general problems in society. This way of viewing school and education started in the nineteenth century, in the wake of the Enlightenment, but it has been intensified since the mid-twentieth century. Tröhler draws attention to a number of specific problems that have triggered national and international school reforms. He mentions, for example, how the launch of the first Russian satellite, Sputnik, in 1958 led to anxiety in the Western world about lagging behind in technological development; this sparked educational reforms with a focus on science, mathematics, and technology. In a similar way, we can see in Sweden how school is held up as the place that will successfully deal with everything from sex to a flexible labor market. Sustainable development is of course no exception, and since the early 1990s school and its pupils and teachers have been in focus when sustainability problems have been discussed (Ideland & Tröhler, 2015). School and societal development, in other words, are closely linked. Thomas Popkewitz (1998) even states that it is impossible to understand school as a phenomenon without linking it to a hope of being able to steer not only family life but also society as a whole.

In our time, then, there is a powerful belief that school can make children and young people "reasonable" (helping them into "the truth" and into the right emotions). Here school is a part of the modern project; society and the future can be planned and steered. This rationalization will tame all that is magical and irrational, decisions and development will be based on reason. Society must be capable of calculation and planning, and therefore knowledge, development, and growth will liberate people and society alike (Bauman, 1996; Weber, 2009). Whether it is possible or not can be discussed, and there are many philosophers, sociologists, anthropologists, historians, and other scholars who have questioned the rationality of modernity, if it exists at all. For instance, Jane Bennett's (2001) book *The Enchantment of Modern Life* points out the need to upset the distinct categorizations of modernity in order to create a new ethics—not least for the environmental movement. Furthermore, Bruno Latour (1993) claims that these distinct categorizations, for instance the separation of nature and human activity, have never been really possible. This is an ideal rather than a societal form. In any case, the ideals of modernity construct conceptions of an ideal person. This can be described as a cosmopolitan citizen living rationally and solving problems, while also being empathetic, inclusive, and tolerant (Popkewitz, 2012); an ideal inside and beyond the ESE discourse, but which is excluding in a double gesture.

The Making of a Book

This book is written from a Swedish perspective, using Swedish empirical material and also discussing the making of Swedishness. Can this be interesting for an international audience? On the one hand: Maybe not. The analysis focuses on how a national identity of the Swede as an environmental hero is historically produced and today (re)produces an idea of Swedishness through knowledge of and engagement in sustainability. On the other hand: Absolutely, since the analysis focuses on how a national identity is historically produced and (re)produces nationalism in the name of a commitment to sustainability. This is an issue not limited to Sweden, but something important to discuss in more general terms; who is included or excluded in the category of environmentally friendly people, and how is it related to class, nationality, and race? Also, the question of children as agents of change for the future is a common theme in transnational educational policy on ESE.

But to give you a bit of the context: Swedish education policy after Second World War—from the late 1940s to the mid-1970s—follows a route of modernization and reorganization in the creation of the Swedish welfare state (Lundahl, 2002). In recent years, however, it has changed and the state project of education is today clearly influenced by transnational edu-policy—as with many other nations' school systems. International assessments, with follow-up reports, steer the political governance of school. Beside an internationalization of school governance, the Swedish system has undergone a neoliberal turn in both an economic and a cultural sense. In economic terms, this is because education today is organized in a hybrid public/private way. The Swedish educational system has gone from a strong welfare state system to what Stephen Ball (2009) would conceptualize as a recalibration of the state into a market. Market orientation was gradually introduced during the 1990s with a growth of "corporate schools," allowing profit for the owners. The marketization and neoliberalization of the educational system is thus not only about earning money, but also about constructing the meanings and practices of schooling and learning. In the knowledge economy, a certain kind of ideal citizen is constructed: the enterprising subject with certain dispositions and knowledge (Olmedo, Bailey, & Ball, 2013). As will be discussed below, this enterprising subject is also a part of the eco-certified child. Furthermore, the marketization of Swedish education has opened up for an increased heterogeneity concerning how to "do" school, and for business actors to provide teaching and learning tools such as teaching material. It is in this context the book must be read.

As an empirical foundation for the book there is a structured selection of material along with examples of a more anecdotal character. Yet it deserves to be pointed out—clearly and emphatically—that what I have studied is texts and pictures that tell of sustainable development and by extension reproduce the figuration of the eco-certified child. I have not observed any "real people" of flesh and blood. What happens when these texts and pictures land in classrooms, on kitchen tables, in people's thoughts and actions I have not studied. The cultural theses of the eco-certified child is almost certainly renegotiated, adjusted to a person's own everyday life and value system. Despite this, I think that the discourse is interesting because it costs to go against normality. We know that it steers how we *can* teach, learn, feel, act, and live in an environmentally friendly way.

In the research project "The Eco-certified Child" we examined teaching material and policy documents aimed at preschool and school. Policy documents include, for example, Swedish curricula and syllabuses (from 1962, 1969, 1980, 1994, and 2011).[6] In all of them, teaching about the environment has been emphasized and steered in some form, depending on the spirit of the time. In the 1960s it was above all about nature conservancy in the local community, but since the 1980 curriculum there has been a global perspective, and since 1994 there has been a clear link to *Agenda 21* and sustainable development. During the last few decades there has also been a culturally elevated focus on the individual's personal consumption choices (Hillbur et al., 2016). One of the four fundamental perspectives in the curriculum for Swedish compulsory school is the environment, and the presentation of that is a good illustration of how personal and global perspectives interact:

> An environmental perspective provides opportunities not only to take responsibility for the environment in areas where they themselves can exercise direct influence, but also to form a personal position with respect to overarching and global environmental issues. Teaching should

---

[6]See Kungliga Skolöverstyrelsen (1962), Skolöverstyrelsen (1969, 1980), Skolverket (1994, 2011).

illuminate how the functions of society and our ways of living and working can best be adapted to create sustainable development. (National Agency for Education, 2011, p. 12)

The category of policy documents also includes international documents such as the UN *Agenda 21* (UN, 1992) and *Our Common Future* (UN, 1987), and *the Stockholm Declaration* (UN, 1972). Also belonging to this category are the websites of the different UN agencies, UNESCO and UNEP, on the theme of education for sustainable development, and the policy of environmental organizations and corporations for education in environment and sustainability. In short, the policy material describes what should be done in the project to "save the world." The documents formulate what is considered a problem, and proposes solutions to it by pointing out the actions, knowledge, and abilities that are necessary for the purpose.

The most important empirical foundation for the book is the teaching material that has been analyzed. To provide a bit of context here: textbooks in Swedish schools are not published or controlled by the state. These are instead published by commercial companies, and it is up to each school to decide whether the teaching material helps to achieve the goals stated in the curriculum and the syllabus. This means that different schools work with different types of material which can come from commercial publishers but also from interest organizations and businesses. At present the Swedish National Agency for Education is working to produce modules for teaching about environment and sustainability, which can best be described as guidance for teachers in their teaching and assessment.

In other words, the teaching material studied varies somewhat in character. I would nevertheless claim that the discourse (re)produced in it is very much the same as regards content, but there are great differences in the design. Some material is geared to conveying knowledge, some seeks to engage and activate pupils. First of all, there are the classical textbooks produced by commercial publishers for the different levels of compulsory school. It is chiefly books for the upper level (7–9th grade) that have more detailed texts about sustainability and environment. The school subjects that deal with issues of sustainability are science subjects (biology, physics, chemistry) and social science subjects (especially geography and civics), and home economics with consumer education. The approach obviously differs from subject to subject, although there are similarities. All subjects have the goal that the pupil will learn how to make everyday decisions to promote sustainable development. Broadly speaking the science subjects underline the importance of using subject knowledge when making personal and political decisions, while the social science subjects emphasize a societal perspective and home economics focuses more on the individual's consumption and good housekeeping.[7]

School teaching material about sustainable development goes far beyond traditional textbooks. Many feel called upon to help, which also confirms the thesis that it is through education that the world can be changed. Keep Sweden Clean (Håll Sverige Rent), the Swedish Society for Nature Conservation (Naturskyddsföreningen), and the World Wide Fund for Nature (WWF) are three major players on the market. They work with certification of schools and preschools and build up model schools for sustainable development. Their material has been analyzed by the project, the WWF material from a historical angle as well. Alongside the environmental organizations, the business NGO Confederation of Swedish Enterprise (Svenskt Näringsliv) has published educational material, as have companies with a desire to help schools to save the world. Another place where the figure of the eco-certified child appears is in educational games (digital and analog), apps, children's books, and puzzles. These too have been analyzed.

Having noted this, I want to make it clear that the research project on which I have worked for a number of years has not made any distinction between different teaching materials. There was no ambition, nor even any wish, to investigate whether the material is correct or can help to achieve the goals. Policy texts, commercially published books, the material from the Confederation of Swedish Enterprise, the games, and even research articles have all been analyzed in the same way, as places where the discourse about sustainable life and the eco-certified child is

---

[7]Read more about the Swedish policy documents in Hillbur et al. (2016).

(re)produced and the figuration of the eco-certified child is made. One consequence of this is that, in this book, I have not stated the names of the authors of the texts; instead I refer to them by the title or by the name of the organization behind them. This might seem as if I do not ascribe sufficient significance to the authors, but I want to shift the focus from individual persons and texts to the discourse—possible ways of thinking and talking about sustainability, the environment, and eco-certified children. I am thus interested in discursive *effects* rather than individual senders and their motives.[8] What do the texts do with the notion of the good life and the dangerous life, desirable and problematic people? How are the eco-certified child and the Other formulated in these texts?

So much concerning the material aimed at school. In the work on this book I have also tried to look outside the educational system, in search of the eco-certified person who is not necessarily a child or a pupil. This search is far from being structured or all-embracing; instead it follows the idea of trying to track a question through different contexts rather than conducting a comprehensive study of a limited area. Inspired by George Marcus's (1995) notion of multi-sited ethnography, conceptualizing how the researcher follows a question rather than a specific, delimited place and time, this study can therefore best be described as a multi-sited desk study. It aims to put pieces together, to understand and deconstruct the figuration of the eco-certified child. Hereby, I also draw on Richardson and St Pierre's (2008) work on "writing" as a method of inquiry. That means that I try to "to find something out" through reading and writing, to draw lines between different sources from both inside and outside the context of education.

My theoretical point of departure, as described above, is that the truth about desirable and problematic people is made by defining what is reason and a reasonable way of life, "the reason of reason" (Popkewitz, 2009). A truth like this tends not to be confined to school, being rather a discourse organizing society as a whole. This search, however, has mainly been intended to give a deeper understanding of the school discourse constructing the figuration of the eco-certified child, rather than

---

[8]Their names are however to be found in the reference list.

to survey alternative fields. This means that I have, above all, gone to "places" that (re)produce the same figuration, for example, advertising and movies. As a result—for better or worse—the eco-certified child sketched in the book is relatively unambiguous. Of course there are alternative discourses and figures, at other "places" in society, which no doubt find their way into school as well, in other ways than via the teaching material. Environmental engagement is strong and multifaceted. Within the environmental movement we find veganism, barter economies, political activism, and so on. What is interesting from my perspective is that these are seldom visible in the school material that I have studied. On the contrary, they can be excluded by being defined as ideological, fundamentalist, irresponsible, unreliable, or greedy—outside of and a threat to "the truth" (Foucault, 1971). For instance, the political activist can be portrayed in the school material as the Other instead of the environmentally friendly person. I shall return later to how this is done.

Outline of the Book

This introduction is followed by chapters outlining a cultural protocol for the eco-certified child, and how this (re)produces taken-for-granted understandings of race, nationalities, and social class. Chapter 2, analyzes and problematizes how a neoliberal ideology organizes the ESE discourse and the figuration of the eco-certified child, that is to say, how the individual choice is elevated, and how individuals become accountable for solving environmental problems through consumer power. The responsibility for the survival of the world is internalized in children since everyday choices are attached to global issues. Besides the problem with the fact that small children are made accountable for political issues, this discourse requires us to do sustainability work individually—I would claim at the cost of overall political reforms. By applying Foucault's notion of pastoral power I point out how ESE operates as a governing technology by constructing humankind as in need of salvation and reaching this through sacrifices. This is done through pointing out the individual as responsible not only for him/herself, but also for the flock now and in the future.

Chapter 3, explores how the figuration of the eco-certified child is (re)produced inside a cultural politics of emotions. Also the former chapter discusses emotions in relation to individualism, but this chapter focuses on how emotions are seen as connected to knowledge; how the "right" knowledge and skills contribute to the "right emotions." The chapter also deconstructs how an "optimization of emotions" in and through ESE is supposed to happen, and how "doing" things has become a way to push away "bad feelings" such as anxiety and anger over an unjust and unsustainable world. Through a kind of activation of the eco-certified child, s/he is supposed to engage in the world with a good mood—which makes ESE into a "nice" practice avoiding complex problems as well as anger, despair, or apathy. Hence, the analysis also examines how the enlightened person is represented through whiteness; how coloniality, in terms of Western enlightenment organizes the ESE discourse and the figuration of the child.

Chapter 4, deepens the analysis of how Us and Them are constructed through a colonial understanding of the world, and how this is embedded in the field of ESE. A running theme is to analyze how sustainability engagement has a nationalistic touch, and how the different positioning of humans living in different parts of the world constructs an enlightened, organized Us in the Global North and a miserable, corrupt, under-developed Them in the Global South (McClintock, 1995). Besides this (re)production of the eco-certified child and its Other in terms of nationality and geography, the issue of race is in focus. In the Swedish discourse the enlightened, helping environmental hero is always represented by a white person, while those who are in need of help are represented by a person of color. An often-silenced theme is the fact that the countries described as exceptional at sustainability actually have huge ecological footprints (e.g. Sweden, Denmark). Yet these countries are described as "world champions in sustainability." The chapter discusses how this can be possible, and how environmental engagement has become culturally attached to whiteness and a Western lifestyle. The work for a common future has, ironically, become an excluding practice dividing the world in Us and Them.

Chapter 5, continues to examine how the environmentally friendly person becomes culturally attached to a place—in the former chapter it was a certain nation or part of the globe, in this nature as a welcoming or excluding place is discussed. It focuses on the figuration of the eco-certified child as a nature-loving person—the one who likes being outdoors in all weather, discovering and caring for nature. Nature becomes a metaphorical place organizing desirable and undesirable ways of living, and it is attached to a certain subjectivity entangled in cultural norms for race and class. For instance, the "use" of nature in the Swedish ESE discourse is (re)produces a middle-class way of living as desirable, with weekend excursions out into the field. But another "use" is that nature is a place for learning—which contributes to the construction of the modern, reasonable, child. With help from Nirmal Puwar's book *Space Invaders* (2004), I discuss how different places—the sacral nature and the urban ghetto—are culturally attached to a specific kind of people, and how the ones crossing the borders become "space invaders," disturbing the community.

The final Chapter 6, studies the consequences of individualization and nationalistic approaches to sustainability and how these rationalities organize what is seen as reason as well as the reasonable, desirable children who engage in environment and sustainability in a proper way. Furthermore, this chapter focuses on how the child is constructed in and through this discourse; how the child becomes the representative of the pure, untouched soul—still not destroyed by the cynicism of the adult world. The figuration of the eco-certified child as an agent of change and the hope for the future is analyzed and problematized. Here I also discuss alternative ways of talking about environment and sustainability, and how other perspectives can redistribute the responsibility for the future from childhood into the political arena.

References

Adichie, C. N. (2009). *The danger of a single story*. Ted Talks. http://www.ted.com/talks/chimamanda_adichie_the_danger_of_a_single_story?language=en.

Ahmed, S. (2004). Affective economies. *Social Text, 22*(2), 117–139.

Ahmed, S. (2010). *The promise of happiness*. Durham: Duke University Press.

Ahmed, S. (2014). *The cultural politics of emotion* (2nd ed.). Edinburgh: Edinburgh University Press.

Arendt, H. (1963). *Eichmann in Jerusalem: A report on the banality of evil.* New York, NY: Penguin.

Ball, S. J. (2009). Privatising education, privatising education policy, privatising educational research: Network governance and the 'competition state'. *Journal of Education Policy, 24*(1), 83–99.

Bauman, Z. (1996). *Postmodern etik.* Göteborg: Daidalos.

Bengtsson, S., & Östman, L. (2013). Globalisation and education for sustainable development: Emancipation from context and meaning. *Environmental Education Research, 19*(4), 477–498.

Bennett, J. (2001). *The enchantment of modern life: Attachments, crossings, and ethics.* Princeton, NJ: Princeton University Press.

Billig, M. (1999). Conversation analysis and the claims of naivety. *Discourse & Society, 10*(4), 572–576.

Brown, W. (2006). *Regulating aversion: Tolerance in the age of identity and empire.* Princeton, NJ: Princeton University Press.

Butler, J. (1993). *Bodies that matter: On the discursive limits of 'sex'.* New York, NY: Routledge.

Carter, R. G. (2006). Of things said and unsaid: Power, archival silences, and power in silence. *Archivaria, 61,* 215–233.

Castañeda, C. (2002). *Figurations: Child, bodies, worlds.* Durham: Duke University Press.

Castro-Gómez, S. (2002). The social sciences, epistemic violence, and the problem of the "invention of the other". *Nepantla: Views from South, 3*(2), 269–285.

Dyer, R. (1993). The matter of images. *Essays on representations.* New York, NY: Routledge.

Dyer, R. (1997). *White.* New York, NY: Routledge.

Edmondson, B. (2014). *Ice cream social: The struggle for the Soul of Ben & Jerry's.* San Fransisco: Berrett-Koehler.

Essed, P. (1991). *Understanding everyday racism: An interdisciplinary theory.* Newbury Park, CA: Sage.

Foucault, M. (1971). *Orders of discourse: Social science information, 10*(2), 7–30.

Foucault, M. (1980). *Power/knowledge: Selected interviews and other writings 1972–1977* (C. Gordon, Ed.). Harlow: Harvester Press.

Foucault, M. (1983). The subject and power. In H. Dreyfus & P. Rabinow (Eds.), *Michel Foucault: Beyond structuralism and hermeneutics* (pp. 208–226). Chicago, IL: University of Chicago Press.

Foucault, M. (1990). *The History of Sexuality* (Vol. 1). New York: Vintage Books.

Foucault, M. (1991). Governmentality. In G. Burchell, C. Gordon, & P. Miller (Eds.), *The Foucault effect: Studies in governmentality* (pp. 87–104). Chicago, IL: University of Chicago Press.

Foucault, M., Senellart, M., & Davidson, A. I. (2007). *Security, territory, population*. Basingstoke: Palgrave Macmillan.

Fröhlich, G., Sellmann, D., & Bogner, F. X. (2013). The influence of situational emotions on the intention for sustainable consumer behaviour in a student-centred intervention. *Environmental Education Research, 19*(6), 747–764.

González-Gaudiano, E. (2005). Education for sustainable development: Configuration and meaning. *Policy Futures in Education, 3*(3), 243–250.

Gough, S., & Scott, W. (2006). Education and sustainable development: A political analysis. *Educational Review, 58*(3), 273–290.

Hacking, I. (1995). The looping effects of human kinds. *Causal cognition: A multidisciplinary debate, 12*, 351–394.

Hacking, I. (2006). Making up people. *London Review of Books 28*(16), 3–26.

Hall, S. (1992). The west and the rest: Discourse and power. In S. Hall & B. Geiben (Eds.), *Formations of modernity* (pp. 15–30). Cambridge, UK: Polity Press.

Haraway, D. J. (2004). *The Haraway reader*. New York: Routledge.

Haraway, D. J. (2016). *Staying with the trouble: Making kin in the Chthulucene*. Durham: Duke University Press.

Hillbur, P., Ideland, M., & Malmberg, C. (2016). Response and responsibility: Fabrication of the eco-certified citizen in Swedish curricula 1962–2011. *Journal of Curriculum Studies, 48*(3), 409–426.

Hursh, D., Henderson, J., & Greenwood, D. (2015). Environmental education in a neoliberal climate. *Environmental Education Research, 21*(3), 299–318.

Håkansson, M., Östman, L., & Van Poeck, K. (2018). The political tendency in environmental and sustainability education. *European Educational Research Journal, 17*(1), 91–111.

Ideland, M. (2017). The end of the world and a promise of happiness: Environmental education within the cultural politics of emotions. In T. Popkewitz, J. Diaz, & C. Kirchgasler (Eds.), *A political sociology of educational knowledge: Studies of exclusions and difference*. London: Taylor & Francis.

Ideland, M., & Tröhler, D. (2015). Calling for sustainability: WWF's global agenda and educating Swedish exceptionalism. In D. Tröhler & T. Lenz (Eds.), *Trajectories in the development of modern school systems: Between the national and the global* (pp. 199–212). Abingdon and New York: Routledge.

Jickling, B., & Wals, A. E. (2008). Globalization and environmental education: Looking beyond sustainable development. *Journal of Curriculum Studies, 40*(1), 1–21.

Kopnina, H. (2012). Education for sustainable development (ESD): The turn away from 'environment'in environmental education? *Environmental Education Research, 18*(5), 699–717.

Kopnina, H., & Cherniak, B. (2016). Neoliberalism and justice in education for sustainable development: A call for inclusive pluralism. *Environmental Education Research, 22*(6), 827–841.

Kramming, K. (2017). *Miljökollaps eller hållbar framtid?: Hur gymnasieungdomar uttrycker sig om miljöfrågor.* Uppsala: Uppsala University. Diss.

Kulick, D. (2005). The importance of what gets left out. *Discourse Studies, 7*(4–5), 615–624.

Ladson-Billings, G. (1998). Just what is critical race theory and what's it doing in a nice field like education? *International Journal of Qualitative Studies in Education, 11*(1), 7–24.

Latour, B. (1993). *We have never been modern.* Cambridge: Harvard University Press.

Lloro-Bidart, T. (2017). Neoliberal and disciplinary environmentality and 'sustainable seafood' consumption: Storying environmentally responsible action. *Environmental Education Research, 23*(8), 1182–1199.

Luke, T. W. (1999). Environmentality as green governmentality. In E. Darier (Ed.), *Discourses of the environment* (pp. 121–151). Malden, MA: Blackwell.

Lundahl, L. (2002). From centralisation to decentralisation: Governance of education in Sweden. *European Educational Research Journal, 1*(4), 625–636.

Mannion, G., Biesta, G., Priestley, M., & Ross, H. (2011). The global dimension in education and education for global citizenship: Genealogy and critique. *Globalisation, Societies and Education, 9*(3–4), 443–456.

Marcus, G. E. (1995). Ethnography in/of the world system: The emergence of multi-sited ethnography. *Annual Review of Anthropology, 24*(1), 95–117.

McClintock, A. (1995). *Imperial leather: Race, gender and sexuality in the colonial contest.* New York, NY: Routledge.

McKenzie, M., Bieler, A., & McNeil, R. (2015). Education policy mobility: Reimagining sustainability in neoliberal times. *Environmental Education Research, 21*(3), 319–337.

Nadesan, M. H. (2010). *Governing childhood into the 21st century: Biopolitical technologies of childhood management and education.* New York: Palgrave Macmillan.

National Agency for Education [Skolverket]. (2011). *Curriculum for the compulsory school, preschool class and the recreation centre 2011*. Stockholm: Swedish National Agency for Education.

Öhman, J. (2006). Pluralism and criticism in environmental education and education for sustainable development: A practical understanding. *Environmental Education Research, 12*(2), 149–163.

Ojala, M. (2013). Emotional awareness: On the importance of including emotional aspects in education for sustainable development (ESD). *Journal of Education for Sustainable Development, 7*(2), 167–182.

Olmedo, A., Bailey, P. L., & Ball, S. J. (2013). To infinity and beyond…: Heterarchical governance, the teach for all network in Europe and the making of profits and minds. *European Educational Research Journal, 12*(4), 492–512.

Otieno, C., Spada, H., Liebler, K., Ludemann, T., Deil, U., & Renkl, A. (2014). Informing about climate change and invasive species: How the presentation of information affects perception of risk, emotions, and learning. *Environmental Education Research, 20*(5), 612–638.

Palmer, J. A. (1998). *Environmental education in the 21st century: Theory, practice, progress and promise*. London: Routledge.

Popkewitz, T. S. (1998). *Struggling for the soul: The politics of schooling and the construction of the teacher*. New York: Teachers College Press.

Popkewitz, T. S. (2009). Curriculum study, curriculum history, and curriculum theory: The reason of reason. *Journal of Curriculum studies, 41*(3), 301–319.

Popkewitz, T. S. (2012). *Cosmopolitanism and the age of school reform: Science, education, and making society by making the child*. Abingdon and New York: Routledge.

Puwar, N. (2004). *Space invaders, race, gender and bodies out of place*. New York: Berg.

Richardson, L., & St. Pierre, E. (2008). A method of inquiry. *Collecting and Interpreting Qualitative Materials, 3*(4), 473.

Rose, N., & Miller, P. (2010). Political power beyond the state: Problematics of government. *The British Journal of Sociology, 61*, 271–303.

Said, E. (1978). *Orientalism: Western representations of the Orient*. New York: Pantheon.

Serder, M., & Ideland, M. (2016). PISA truth effects: The construction of low performance. *Discourse: Studies in the Cultural Politics of Education, 37*(3), 341–357.

Skolverket. (1994), *Läroplan för det obligatoriska skolväsendet, förskoleklassen och fritidshemmet Lpo 94.* Stockholm: Skolverket.

Skolverket. (2011). *Läroplan för grundskolan, förskoleklassen och fritidshemmet 2011.* Stockholm: Skolverket.

Skolöverstyrelsen. (1969). *Läroplan för grundskolan.* Stockholm: Svenska utbildningsförlaget Liber.

Skolöverstyrelsen. (1980). *Läroplan för grundskolan, Lgr 80.* Stockholm: Liber.

Soneryd, L., & Uggla, Y. (2015). Green governmentality and responsibilization: New forms of governance and responses to 'consumer responsibility'. *Environmental Politics, 24*(6), 913–931.

Spivak, G. C. (1988). Can the subaltern speak? In C. Nelson & L. Grossberg (Eds.), *Marxism and the interpretation of culture* (pp. 271–313). Basingstoke, UK: Macmillan Education.

The Royal National Board of Education [Kungliga skolöverstyrelsen]. (1962). *Läroplan för grundskolan* [Curriculum for the compulsory school]. Stockholm: Kungliga skolöverstyrelsen.

Tröhler, D. (2009). Harmonizing the educational globe: World polity, cultural features, and the challenges to educational research. *Studies in Philosophy and Education, 29*(1), 7–29.

Tröhler, D. (2011). *Languages of education: Protestant legacies, national identities, and global aspirations.* New York: Routledge.

UN. (1972). *Declaration of the United Nations conference on the human environment.* New York: United Nations.

UN. (1987). *Report of the World Commission on Environment and Development: Our common future.* New York: United Nations.

UN. (1992). *Agenda 21.* New York: United Nations.

Weber, M. (2009). *From Max Weber: Essays in sociology.* Abingdon: Routledge.

2

Free-Range Children

Abstract The chapter problematizes how a neoliberal ideology organizes Environmental and Sustainability Education (ESE) and the figuration of the eco-certified child. The chapter illuminates how the individual choice is elevated in the sustainability discourse, and how individuals become accountable for solving global problems. The focus of individual choices is understood from Foucault's theories on pastoral power: how ESE operates through describing humankind as in need of salvation. This is done through pointing out the individual as responsible for not only oneself, but also the "flock." As well, the use of numbers is problematized: how tables, footprints, and numerical comparisons make different ways of handling sustainability problems possible respectively impossible. The chapter ends with emphasizing the need for politicizing the individualism in ESE.

Keywords Pastoral power · Neoliberalism · Sustainability discourse

"Save the world a little every day." This is an advertising slogan for the Swedish eco-label *the Swan*. As a background to the text there are pictures that are at once frightening and beautiful. Forest fires, parched

© The Author(s) 2019   **31**
M. Ideland, *The Eco-Certified Child*, Palgrave Studies in Education
and the Environment, https://doi.org/10.1007/978-3-030-00199-5_2

soil, oil slicks, smoke rising from a factory stack against a gray sky, and a sewage pipe discharging into what looks like the sea. The message is clear: the world is threatened but it can be saved by our joint efforts, even if they are small. The Swan website (svanen.se) tells us more about the campaign, where the message is even more explicit:

> The Swan makes exacting demands on products and services as regards environment, health, and quality. License holders change their production, modify their working routines, and change ingredients to meet our demands. Now it is up to you to show that you support our work for a better environment. Of course the Swan alone cannot save the world. But you, we, and our license holders contribute what we can. For your choices, our choices, and everyone's choices do in fact make a difference. Thank you for helping to save the world a little every day! #raddavarlden. (http://www.svanen.se/radda-varlden/)

The end of this exhortation, "For your choices, our choices, and everyone's choices do in fact make a difference," is a good summary of how the sustainability discourse focuses both on individuals and on "everyone" at the same time. The message is that we all must do our little bit and that the eco-certified person is someone who is constantly aware that every little choice he or she makes every day is significant. Everything counts. But it is done of free will, because the eco-certified child is "free-range." You can "choose" to switch off the light when you leave the room, or "choose" to leave it on. You "choose" to shower for a long time or you make a more environmentally friendly "choice" and take a quick shower. Not least of all, it counts whether you "choose" the eco-labeled product or something else which may be much cheaper, one that you can better afford. But how come this free choice has been elevated into the solution to our problems?

In the theoretical tradition outlined in the previous chapter, where the governing of people's actions is said to take place through definitions of normality and deviation, free choice has a very special meaning. In the book *Inventing Our Selves* (1998), the sociologist Nikolas Rose writes about how people's freedom is achieved not only by being "free to choose" but also by being "forced to be free." Environmental problems and their solutions should be understood in terms of individuals' choice of lifestyle, and that is why the individual can feel that he or she is saving the world (a little) by buying one product instead of another. As a textbook in ESE observes:

> IT IS YOUR CHOICE!
> A sustainable environment in the future is dependent on the choices people like you and I make. We have the possibility to change our way of living and get other people to realize how important these issues are. If we take our mission seriously a sustainable future is perfectly possible. (Bowden, 2005, p. 45)

But how free is the choice? Rose also writes that a core element in today's advanced liberal society is to get people to make the choices that suit a specific political rationality based on individualism and capitalism—two cornerstones of the neoliberal social imaginary that pervade society as a whole, including schools and ESE (Hursh, Henderson, & Greenwood, 2015; Rizvi & Lingard, 2010). As we saw in the last chapter, the right choices are the ones that are the same as "the general will," as the ongoing political project. This means that, just like the free-range hen or pig, we are ultimately enclosed within certain frames. Not all choices are possible at the same time if you want to stay within the limits of "the truth."

Rose (1998) studies psychological tests and how they are organized by discourses about the way in which people are supposed to act. In other words, it is a highly individual-focused practice he is studying. One could imagine that the discourse about sustainable development looks different because here it is "the environment" and "the world" that are the objects to be saved. But an image that recurs time and again in the material I have studied is how the globe rests in a person's hands. It is the human individual that holds the fate of the world, not the other way around. In a way this is a good illustration of the Anthropocene, that the ecological system has changed because of human influence, rather than stressing the interaction between different species—which Donna Haraway (2016) holds up as essential. But the pictures of the globe in human hands probably do not allude to the deeper ethical and ecological meaning, but rather seek to inculcate that people must assume their responsibility; the individual must learn to make better free choices.[1] In the rhetoric about "everyone" and the shared responsibility, it is still the individual that is singled out as the agent of change. This agent of change is not defined by his or her circumstances but by his or her choices. That idea derives partly from a psychological theory of decision-making that grew in the West after the Second World War. Human nature did not seem rational enough, so the system for choices became a way to steer and organize society. A new science of choices grew, focusing on the choice rather than the chooser. Hector Heyck (2012) states that this was seen as the ultimate tool for organizing a modern, advanced liberal society.

The significance of "choice" returns over and over again, in society and in school teaching material and other texts and images aimed at children. Checklists, calculators, estimates of different kinds are powerful governing technologies which can tell you in numbers how you and your choices fit the sustainability project (Andrée, Hansson, & Ideland, 2018; Ideland & Malmberg, 2015). In Rose's (1998, p. 121) words, we can call them centers of calculation in which good behavior and debts to the world and the future can be calculated and made visible. In this chapter, I want to show how these centers of calculation do not only calculate but also govern by (re)producing an eco-certified person who seemingly makes rational and logical choices, based on facts and statistics. They speak with the voice of expertise and according to Peter Miller (2004), calculative practices should be analyzed as "mechanisms through which programs of government are articulated and made operable" (p. 179). In general, the numbers that appear in the results are seen as objective and indisputable and function as a way of depoliticizing the political by making them appear objective. Numbers appear to safeguard against political will and cultural differences (Rose 1991).

---

[1] This discussion continues in the chapter "Natural—With No Artificial Additives."

Footprints and Promises to the Future

In the sustainability discourse the calculation of ecological footprints has made a big impact during the twenty-first century, and it is used as a tool in ESE. Studies show that education that uses climate or ecological footprints increases the motivation for pro-environmental behavior (e.g. Cooke, Fielding, & Louis, 2016; Gottlieb, Vigoda-Gadot, & Haim, 2013; Lin, 2016; Typhina, 2017). The idea is in many ways brilliant: based on the world's natural resources/biocapacity and population, the area of the earth's surface available to each person (if the world were fair) is calculated. This is called a global hectare (GHA). With this model one can calculate and display whether nations and individuals over- or underconsume the earth's resources. Moreover, one can calculate at what point in the year we have used up the earth's resources, and start nibbling at next year's—thus running into debt. "The earth" is (re)produced and understood in an economic discourse about the possibilities of saving or squandering.

At the "top" of the league of nations with large ecological footprints are the oil countries with relatively small populations, such as the United Arab Emirates, Bahrain, and Qatar (all over 10 GHA/person)—but also the Nordic countries (including Sweden, 5.88 GHA/person), the USA, Canada, and Australia. At the "bottom" are poor countries such as Malawi, Afghanistan, and Timor (about 0.5 GHA/person). Similar lists, with telling numbers, exist for things such as CO_2 emissions calculated as tonnes per capita.

Countries ranked by ecological footprint per capita (in global hectares)
1. Qatar 15.7
2. Luxembourg 12.3
3. United Arab Emirates 9.8
4. Mongolia 9.5
5. Bahrain 8.7
6. United States of America 8.4
7. Canada 8.0
8. Kuwait 7.6

9. Denmark 7.1
10. Estonia 7.0
11. Australia 6.9
12. Bermuda 6.8
13. Belgium 6.7
14. Trinidad and Tobago 6.7
15. Sweden 6.6
16. Aruba 6.4
17. Oman 6.3
18. Finland 6.1
19. Norway 6.0
20. Saudi Arabia 6.0
(data retrieved from http://data.footprintnetwork.org/#/)

The figures confirm and (re)produce an established narrative about poor and rich countries. To a certain extent they also (re)produce established truths about environmental villains and environmental heroes, but to some extent these taken-for-granted truths are contradicted. The United States is a country which, at least in the Swedish discourse, tends to be singled out as one of the worst environmental "villains" (side by side with China). But in the table above Denmark comes right after the United States in the "league of villains," and Sweden is not far behind. From my Swedish perspective, Denmark and Sweden are nations with a strong identity as environmentally friendly, keen to sell the nation's trademarks using images of bicycles, wind turbines, and billowing fields of grain. In other words, the national symbolic values do not correspond to calculations of ecological footprints. Of course, things are not as simple as the list above suggests. Sweden, for example, tops a much more flattering list ranking the countries where the most sustainable production of goods takes place. This means that Swedes consume imported goods that are produced in wretched circumstances, but keeps its own backyard relatively clean. This suits well for maintaining a national identity as environmentally friendly. The complexity, however, is rarely seen in teaching material about the environment and sustainability. On the contrary, what emerges from texts and pictures—inside and outside the Swedish school system—is a rather uniform discourse about

Swedish exceptionalism in the environmental field. Nina Witoszek (2018) described Norwegian textbooks in a similar but not an identical way when she studies what is ESD in Norway—"the best country in the world":

> There are many indications that in the twenty-first century, Norwegians have become particularly adept at cultivating cognitive dissonance—i.e. accepting Norway's status as a "mecca of environmentalism" *and* as a successful, even "virtuous" oil economy which generates both unprecedented and relatively fairly distributed social welfare and affluence. The Norwegian curriculum reflects these tensions and paradoxes. (Witoszek, 2018, p. 4)

However, the two identities of Norway—the mecca of environmentalism and the oil-producing nation—are rarely discussed together. They are held separate, as in the Swedish material, and probably also in many other national contexts. In other words, the numbers are used to confirm rather than challenge established images.

The figures for the ecological footprints, as in similar calculations, indicate problems for the world and risks for a sustainable future. These risks, as in the list above, can be nations, but individuals can also calculate their own ecological footprints. On the WWF website, you can find out as an individual: "how many planets would be needed if everyone lived like you. Test our climate-smart calculator to find the answer" (www.wwf.se). In this way you can gain insight, through figures and color pictures, into the type of person you are, eco-certified or dangerous—someone who makes the world a better place or a worse place. Let me tell you about my own result, which showed that if everyone lived as I do, it would take 3.18 copies of our earth. This is illustrated by 3.18 planets. My ecological footprint is 5.72 GHA (the average Swede has 6.4) and my carbon dioxide emission is 11.61 tonnes (compared with 9.3 for the average Swede). This is what I obtained by giving detailed answers to questions about my housing, travel, electricity contract, waste sorting, food choices, how much money I spend on my pets (not what I buy), beauty products (not what kind), and machine tools (interesting example from a gender point of view). It can be revealed that I have been given slightly different figures on different occasions when

I have taken the questionnaire, sometimes above the average, sometimes below. So the actual numbers should be taken with a pinch of salt; it is what they do to us that is interesting. For it did not look good: 3.18 planets—for a person who tries to stand up for sustainability, justice, and equality in my profession and in my political convictions as well as when I buy food. I can't live like this! I feel the shame growing in my body. The link between my small everyday choices and the large global issues is immediate. Through this calculation center, it is not just the nation but also I as an individual that have been made responsible for the survival of the world; my choices are not sustainable and I ought to change if I do not want to belong to the category of the dangerous population. I note, however, that my ecological footprint is smaller than that of the average Swede (probably because I am allergic to gold jewelry and haven't needed to buy a new television set in the last year), but my CO_2 emissions are much greater than "normal."

To understand how these calculations function as governing technologies that operate through our free will, one can consider them with help from Foucault's theory of pastoral power (Foucault, 1983, pp. 213ff.). Even if the power of the church (not the religion but the institution) in the Swedish "modern" secularized society has decreased, it still has its methods for exercising power, albeit in new guises and contexts, yet still with claims to define the truth and to construct people on this basis. Foucault (1983) argues that this specific exercise of power takes place when "each and every one" and "all" are simultaneously pointed out as being responsible. He describes this with the aid of four characteristics. The first is that the ultimate aim of every person's actions is to ensure the individual's salvation in the next life—just as the church uses the places heaven and hell to steer what happens in the present. Characteristic number two is a discourse stating that the individual must be prepared to make sacrifices for the good of the flock. The third characteristic is that power builds on its ability to gain access to people's minds—"the soul" in pastoral language. The way this happens is that people reveal their secrets and thereby expose their innermost being to scrutiny. Power thus operates through conscience. The fourth characteristic of the pastoral exercise of power listed by Foucault is that it is aimed simultaneously at society as a whole and at each individual through all stages of life.

Foucault (1983) himself writes that this might at first sight seem like an outdated historic way of exercising power. But if we apply this outlook to the ecological footprint, and the arguments as to why we should calculate our own, we can see that they function in a similar manner. The truth about sustainable development—its problems and solutions—comes into existence through pastoral power. The next life, for example, can be compared to "future generations." "We do not inherit the earth from our parents, we borrow it from our children" is a common slogan in the discourse. Sustainable *development* is not about life *now* but about the future—the next life (Ideland & Malmberg, 2015). The future as such, as a figure of thought and a metaphor, is in itself an important steering technique—in ESE as in the whole idea about the purpose of education (Hillbur, Ideland, & Malmberg, 2016). Without the idea of needing to secure the future, the truth about sustainability, and hence also the eco-certified person, would have looked different.

The individual's sacrifice for the benefit of the flock is also central in sustainable development, and the climate-smart calculator clearly shows that "you" (which in this case is me) do not sacrifice enough for the flock. Your lifestyle, your consumption must change so that everyone will have room in the earth's global hectare. You must be prepared to make sacrifices! But not too much, and in the right way. You don't have to stop consuming, just consume in the right way. I myself had a relatively small ecological footprint when it came to food because I can buy organic, having a high salary and easy access to it by living in a city. From another life situation, in another national context, the conditions would differ. Another similar test is provided by the energy company Eon to let people measure their carbon dioxide emissions. Since I was able to tick the box for being an Eon customer, and thus consuming non-fossil fuel such as hydroelectric power, the result I obtained was that my emissions are smaller than those of the average citizen of the world. This is despite the fact that I fly all over the world for research conferences and vacations, despite the fact that I have a home that is large and warm and comfortable by global standards, and live with a superabundance of material objects, despite the fact that I have both a car and a dog—two well-known climate villains. But I have chosen to consume electricity from the "right" energy company (according to Eon)[2]—and this choice means that I can feel salvation, unlike my ecological footprint which makes me feel that I must sacrifice more (Andrée et al., 2018). Through self-assessment in sustainability, my life is exposed so that it can be controlled and improved (Lazzarato, 2010; Miller & Rose, 2008, p. 7).

Guilt, Shame and Salvation

There are paths to salvation in this activity, besides choosing a specific company's type of energy. In true pastoral spirit, one can make environmental pledges on the net—a kind of modern letter of indulgence. There you can promise, for example, to take cloth bags to the shop, to pick your own mushrooms, arrange video conferences, eat fewer empty calories, live in a smaller space, and fly direct to the destination without touchdowns (www.minplanet.se). On this website you can see how much carbon dioxide each action saves and how many people have made each pledge. The figures speak clearly. What happens if (or more probably: when) you break the promise is less certain; it is up to your own conscience.

Let us return to Nikolas Rose and his book *Inventing Our Selves*. He writes: "Regulatory systems have sought to codify, calculate, supervise, and maximize the level of functioning of individuals" (Rose, 1998, p. 115). The environmental pledge, dressed in fine words about "making Sweden more climate-smart" (www.minplanet.se), can be said to have a regulatory effect by codifying simple everyday acts in carbon dioxide emissions, calculating how much you can save as an individual; it supervises by defining the good actions (which are sometimes difficult to understand in terms of carbon dioxide emissions, for example, eating fruit instead of "empty calories") and defining how one can maximize

[2]A large proportion of Eon's energy comes from hydroelectric power, which is not fossil fuel and thus does not have the same greenhouse effect as fuels like oil and coal.

an individual's "climate-smartness." The reward that the individual wins is a better conscience. After having first confessed my guilty secrets (for instance that I fly far too much) in the calculation of my ecological footprint, I can gain salvation here through my pledges—not to some god but to the world and to the future (Ideland & Malmberg, 2015). Besides being a calculation center, one could say that this type of website functions like modern society's confession box.

But what kind of pledges are they? What difference do the actions make (assuming that you keep your promise)? They actually do not entail any great sacrifice for the individual. Instead of pledging not to fly at all, for example, you promise to fly direct to the destination if possible. This limitation of the choices can mean more expensive air travel but no other sacrifice—a typical example of how ideals of consumption and growth color the rhetoric of sustainability and environment and where it is rare for any significance to be attached to individuals' varying financial circumstances. By suggesting and offering alternatives that are slightly better than others, the system itself can be maintained and the discourse of growth can be defended. Sara Ahmed (2012) suggests that we need to talk not only about performative discourses—ways of talking that constructs the reality—but also about non-performative discourses. For example, institutions write and publish equality policy, stating how the institution is committed to gender and race equality. However, Ahmed questions if these documents make a real change, or if they just contribute to hide the real, structural problems which are difficult to grasp. The non-performative discourses thus perform a commitment that might rather contribute to status quo than actual change. In a similar way, one can say that the small details that are elevated in the environmental discourse obscure the big problem, that a small part of the earth's population (including myself) live extremely unsustainable lives. But instead of abandoning ideas about the good life, but also to a high extent economical growth, everywhere and always, we try by small means to show our awareness and insight and thus be able to pass as environmentally friendly individuals. The structural level, on the other hand, is discursively silenced.

The environmental pledge, which comprises everything from cloth bags to air travel, is also an example of how pastoral power works by focusing on *every* individual, *all* the time, in *all* parts of life. Power is exercised through the small details, where nothing is too small to be ignored—not even whether you turn off the tap when you are brushing your teeth or which shampoo you choose in the shop. The Italian sociologist and philosopher Maurizio Lazzarato (2010) writes about how constant guilt feelings are created through the regulation of details in life. In this way people also become steerable, through the need to avoid guilt. Guilt is central to the project of sustainable development. It is provoked by the calculation centers and modern confessionals that dictate the guidelines for the right life. Guilt is also close to feelings of shame, whose role in culture has been analyzed by Sara Ahmed (2004; 2010; 2014a, 2014b). She points out that shame makes us look inwards, toward ourselves, our own emotions and our own position, rather than outwards toward our fellow human beings. Shame contributes to the individualization of culture, and the excuse is more a matter of organizing one's own feelings than of doing something for the other—or in this case: for the world.

In school, guilt and shame are created in more or less obvious ways. Climate-smart calculators, aimed directly at children, adolescents, and school classes, are one such instrument provided for instance by the WWF. Here the pupils not only fill in the type of energy used for heating but also how many kilowatt hours are consumed. This can be compared with the individual climate-smart calculator intended for adults, where I "only" needed to state *whether* I recycled metal and paper—not *how much*. In the school calculator the pupil has to enter the number of kilos per year based on a complex calculation (which of course also must be understood as a learning exercise). In other words, *everything* is counted, with seeming accuracy and hard facts. The calculation results in numbers showing what it would be like if everyone lived as the pupils do. The question of how much they can steer different types of energy, food purchases, and so on still remains. So too does the question of how much guilt they should feel.

Another technique for demonstrating the correct lifestyle, and thereby also creating the conditions for guilt, can be found in material aimed at the smallest children. One example is the children's book *Look After Your Planet* (Child, 2008, Swedish translation *Hjälp vår jord*, 2008) with drawing of the siblings Charlie and Lola (as seen on

TV). The book, which is about how Lola becomes an environmentally friendly citizen by learning about recycling, begins and ends with the reader making promises in order to "help our earth." Examples of things the readers "REALLY ever so definitely promise" to do are:

- Try to remember to turn off the tap when I brush my teeth.
- Not complain if it gets a teeny bit cold and maybe put on a jumper instead.
- Try to recycle things rather than throw them away.
- Switch off the lights when I leave a room.
- Make present and birthday cards for my friends from bits and bobs around the house.
- Try not to beg Mum and Dad for the latest and most extremely good new toy—and donate some of my birthday and Christmas money to charity instead.
- Encourage absolutely all my friends, parents and next door people to reuse plastic bags.
  (Child, 2008)

Obviously it is good to turn off the tap when brushing your teeth, and from the point of view of sustainability, it is easy to see that recycling reduces human consumption of natural resources. Nothing wrong with that. Nor is it wrong to want to make children aware of environmental problems. However, we need to think about what challenges of this type, in the form of checklists, do to small children in the form of delegating guilt and responsibility. What they say is that the eco-certified child is one who is constantly on guard, never relaxing, but always participating in the project "Look After Your Planet." The Danish childhood researcher Jan Kampmann (2004) writes about the ideal watch-what-you-do child, a child with self-control based on what is considered rational and sensible and generally "unchildish."

Kampmann's analysis proceeds from the idea of the competent child, a notion that is strong in educational research, school, and especially preschool and child rearing. The child is regarded not just as a future citizen but as a full member of society with influence on his or her own life and that of other people. Kampmann (2004) highlights examples of how the competent child is expected to be able—and permitted—to take part in the family's day-to-day negotiations about the food that is bought and the indoor temperature the home should have—questions that are often held up in the sustainability discourse. Ascribing competence, participation, and freedom to the child can of course be viewed as positive for the child's socialization into a democratic society. The established order for relations between children and adults builds on a distribution of power, and the idea of the competent child is an exciting challenge to the notion that children are not entitled to autonomy and co-determination—or that they cannot contribute to society, as citizens. It is also a challenge to the theory of developmental psychology that is prevalent in educational contexts, about who can do what and at what age. This is well and good. But freedom and power bring responsibility and make new demands of children to be aware of their choices and act correctly for the sake of the flock—the public good—and the world. Jan Kampmann (2004, p. 530) problematizes the idea of the competent child as a liberated child, arguing instead that this liberation is a way for educationists to colonize childhood[3] by insisting that every action has to be substantiated and well thought out. The competent child has become the person on whom we place the responsibility for the future, an environmental agent whose competence and constant watch-what-you-do attitude is the ideal of the eco-certified person. In this cultural figure, forms of normalization are developed and hence also the exclusion of certain children: of those who do not fit the template for the competent child.

The Magic of Numbers

That numbers do things to us is not news. As we saw above, they have a revelatory effect: they can tell us whether we are living a good—in this case sustainable—life or if we belong to the dangerous population; if we consume more than our "allotted" share of the earth's resources; and

---

[3]Cf. also Bernstein (2001, p. 365).

if we emit more carbon dioxide than we "ought" to. All these points of comparison are of course difficult, not to say impossible, to calculate objectively. Despite this, they have a normalizing and hence also a disciplining effect.

Educational science in recent years has seen the emergence of a critical research field that problematizes the way we are influenced by numbers and ranking lists, for example, the results of PISA, the international student assessment. PISA can definitely be seen as a calculation center. Through the communication of the results showing how different nations compare, the numbers function as a kind of conversion table, turning pupils' results into measurable units that are claimed to be able to reflect and compare the quality of different nations' educational systems. A great deal could be said about this, but this is not the place to look in depth at the problems with PISA. My point here is that the value that a nation manages to achieve in the PISA assessment—for example Sweden's 478[4] or South Korea's 554—and the place assigned in the ranking to the school system—for example Sweden's 37th place or South Korea's 1st place—translates a sophisticated measurement system into a simple truth (Gorur, 2014). Complex problems are reduced to comparable numbers and are made to appear rigorous and objective. Thomas Popkewitz (2011, p. 34) writes that communicating with numbers also seems to exclude demands for other forms of assessment. Rose (1991) discusses statistics and numbers as an ethical technology and rationalizes an ethical approach to the world. Through the objectivity of statistics and numbers, a tool is provided for making ethical judgments which are detached from emotion, passion, and non-reason (cf. Bennett, 2001; Holmberg & Ideland, 2016). The numbers communicate something objective and self-evident; they become "things" that steer both our reflections and our actions. One could say that the numbers are performative; they reveal the status of a nation's school system and the reforms that are "required."[5] As Sam Sellar (2015) puts it,

---

[4]These particular figures come from the PISA test in mathematics for 2012.

[5]See further Cowen (2014), Grek (2009), Ideland (2014), Popkewitz (2011), Simons and Masschelein (2008).

numbers work like emotional triggers, but also serve to weld nations and groups together into "imagined communities," to borrow the words of the sociologist Benedict Anderson (2006). They trigger political processes and plans to maintain pride as a nation of knowledge.

In the field of sustainable development and the environment, countries are also compared with the aid of numbers. The table above showing ecological footprints is a kind of ranking list, singling out and constructing environmental villains and heroes at a national level. They steer by means of the politics of comparison (e.g. Grek, 2009). But what otherwise makes the discourse of sustainable development, and its construction of eco-certified people, different from the competent nations of the PISA discourse is that the sustainability project in school is also geared to a different unit, namely, the individual. It is you/I/he/she that is to be compared and changed. If PISA positions nations and their educational systems in relation to each other, the ESE discourse additionally positions individuals with the aid of numbers. We have seen this in the climate-smart calculators above, but it also takes place through more impersonal—albeit individualized—governing technologies.

The book *Klimatsmart: Din guide till en miljövänligare vardag* ("Climate-Smart: Your Guide to a More Environment-Friendly Life") is full of hints on how to act, linking the individual's actions to issues of global survival. And here too the numbers speak:

> If you replace 25 0.5-liter PET bottles with the same amount of tap water, you save 2 kg of carbon dioxide. And about 250–300 kronor.
> If you replace 2 kg of red peppers (grown in a hothouse) with the same amount of carrots, you save 10 kg of carbon dioxide. And about 50 kronor.
> If you replace 5 kg of beef with the equivalent amount of lentils, you save about 63 kg of carbon dioxide. And about 400 kronor. (Persson, Sjöström, & Johnsson, 2007, p. 41)

And so on. What 63 kilos of carbon dioxide means, and how you "save" it, is not stated. Whose are the kilos? Can this resource be used for something else? Once again we find ourselves in an economic discourse where the numbers steer through their mathematical "exactness," their claim to objectivity, and the fact that we have learned to rely on them. They state in a concrete and simple form what is required of the eco-certified person and thereby create a cultural protocol for, simple but good, everyday actions. They steer what we perceive as environmentally friendly and thus as a good citizen. It is almost always a question of active choices, that you *do* something consciously—such as hanging the washing instead of tumble-drying. It is seldom a matter of anything unconscious or unreflected or perhaps quite simply necessary, such as not being able to afford a large home (and a large area to heat) or not owning so many electronic devices that can be on standby (standby must be one of the most "unnecessary" things that can be imagined in the sustainability discourse). Or simply that some people might hang their washing to dry because they have no tumble dryer. These sometimes unchosen but necessary circumstances are not "counted" on the plus side; they are instead subjected to discursive silence. On the other hand, the "choice" not to buy an expensive, eco-labeled product can be counted on the minus side. Having economic capital, in other words, is a necessary investment in the trademark of "the eco-certified child." Not just anyone has access to that category, and in the next chapter I reason about how the economic capital must be combined with a specific cultural capital, to borrow the terms of the sociologist Pierre Bourdieu (1986). Not consuming natural resources is not sufficient; it must be done consciously and with the right motivation.

Governmentality, Graphs, and Constructions of Reality

The technologies described above, in the form of numbers, comparisons, and confessions, function as governing technologies manufacturing the figuration of the eco-certified child. A closely related technology is the construction of mean values and hence normality (Foucault, 2010). The social sciences and the natural sciences agree in using demographics, statistics, and normal values to define truths about the world and about how people "are" and "should be." These function as objects of comparison for the individuals' choices and ideas about themselves and about others. They also contribute to creating what and who is considered as outside the limits of normality. Diagrams operate in a similar way, often in the form of a time line. In school textbooks, as in general reporting, diagrams serve as an educational tool to show how human behavior and changes in the ecosystem are connected. The climate debate gained momentum in public awareness at the moment when Al Gore, in his film *An Inconvenient Truth* (2006), rode in an elevator to illustrate the massive contemporary increase in human carbon dioxide emissions. The diagram, the scale he used, and the creation of a human population as a category became an effective means of persuasion to make people start talking about the relationship between lifestyle, carbon dioxide emissions, and climate change. We—in this case humanity—bear the guilt and that is why we must change. The graph is easy to understand, it visualizes the destiny of humanity with seeming clarity. It translates quantitative data into possibilities for self-regulation, peeling away the complicated social context. No distinction is made here between individuals; on the contrary, everyone can be included in the project through the creation of a guilty population (Höhler, 2015, p. 90). The curves point toward destruction and cry out for help from "humanity" and from every individual belonging to it (Foucault, 1983). Graphs triggered the twenty-first-century climate debate, as they did in the 1960s and 1970s with the debate about access to natural resources and the limits to growth (Höhler, 2015).

At other times the graph is used to indicate the opposite, a hopeful future. The curve shows how humanity's efforts make a difference in a positive sense. This perspective can be found particularly in the school material on sustainable development produced by the interest organization the Confederation of Swedish Enterprise, *Miljö—så funkar det* ("The Environment—How It Works," 2010). It begins with the heading "Is everything getting worse?" and the following text:

> When you read the newspapers or watch TV today, it is easy to believe that the environmental problems have arisen now and that everything is getting worse. But is that how it really is? To be able to answer, you first have to go back in time and ask the question, were things really better

in the past? What environmental problems existed before we built industries, developed new technology, manufactured cars, and invented substances for plant protection? What is development like today? Has the work on environmental issues yielded results, or was it better in the past? (Svenskt Näringsliv, 2010, p. 4)

The material then aims to show how life and society have become better—thanks to economic and technological development, often illustrated in diagrams showing the following:

- The proportion of undernourished people has decreased.
- The availability of food has increased.
- Sweden's carbon dioxide emissions in relation to the rest of the world have decreased.
- Emissions of nitrogen oxides and sulfur oxides have decreased.
- The Swedish forest is estimated to be growing.
- Sweden tops a list showing the proportion of eco-certified companies.
- Energy consumption by fridges and freezers has decreased.
- Wind power is growing.

No diagram in the material from the Confederation of Swedish Enterprise shows any increase in environmental problems. On the contrary, it is a success story, especially from a Swedish perspective, that is told. Through selected numbers and graphs, Sweden is made into a shining example of modern-day technological, economic, and sustainable development. All that is needed is to continue on this path… The text ends with the words: "It is all the fantastic, inventive people in the world, those who propel development, that make the world into an ever-better place to live in" (Svenskt Näringsliv, 2010, p. 55). Here the enterprising subject is portrayed as saving the world, the good neoliberal subject who fits the idea of capitalism and development. The educational material from the Confederation of Swedish Enterprise is not representative of the discourse, with its strong focus on an improved society and with its lack of disaster scenarios such as climate catastrophes and reduced biodiversity. But it is a good example of how the development discourse is closely associated both with capitalism and with a focus on the individual—rather than the collective—as the main force behind change, that is to say, the neoliberal imagery that characterizes ESE (Hursh et al., 2015). It is not always as obvious as in the material from the Confederation of Swedish Enterprise. On the contrary, the focus on economic development and individualism is veiled through virtually religious language such as "our common future," hope, and salvation. This rather crass economic reasoning stands out as both apolitical and unproblematic. It is presented as the only way to go, the truth, which makes it necessary to problematize.

Eco-Certified, Post-political Numbers

The constructions of reality by Al Gore and the Confederation of Swedish Enterprise have seemingly different effects, steering people in different directions. But in one way they belong to the same discourse, the one that calls on people's willingness to change and personal responsibility to get the shared curves to point in the right direction. They steer by talking to people's souls and their sense of responsibility by highlighting individuals' competence to act and make good choices and connecting this to the fate of the population. Modern society can be calculated, measured, and steered. Max Weber's (2009) interpretation of modernity fits the discourse of sustainability like a glove. The free-range eco-certified person can save the world in the name of rationality, unlike the unengaged, unwilling, and dangerous population, those who do not even take the objective numbers seriously, regardless of the environmental effects the different lifestyles actually have.

The objective numbers in combination with the exercise of pastoral power with a focus on the future obscure structural injustices and people's different environmental debts and their need to change. By simultaneously pointing out each and every person, probably often out of a wish to include and not to make distinctions, a specific group in society—the well-off urban middle class—becomes the norm for how the eco-certified person ought to live. This is a person who can make consumer choices, both for economic reasons and from having an almost infinite range of goods and services to choose from. Another perspective, with other numbers and with a focus on different groups in society, could reveal injustices. Numbers of a different type could leave the individual level, and the individual's power, behind, in favor of a willingness to affect the environment politically. Naomi Klein, for example, uses a different type of numbers as a governing technology to persuade people about an alternative worldview in her book *This Changes Everything: Capitalism vs. the Climate* (2015). Among other things, the reader is told that the amount of carbon that the energy companies say they need to have "in reserve" corresponds to a value of 27 billion US dollars and that the oil and gas industry spends 400,000 US dollars a day lobbying in the American Congress (Klein, 2015, pp. 148f.). These figures do not indicate the individual's sacrifice but the political structure and the problem of capitalism. A figure of 27 billion dollars talks to my soul, but in a completely different language than the statement that my consumption needs 3.18 planets. It talks to me as a political being rather than a consumer.

The political scientist Chantal Mouffe (2011) and others argue that the post-political attitude is a negative effect of global capitalism and a neoliberal ideology that puts individual choices before collective solutions.[6] Responsibility is demanded after the event, not through rules—the king has been beheaded, as in the metaphor we saw in the introduction. It is also this society that Nikolas Rose, among others, has described as advanced liberal, which is steered through personal responsibility, guilt, and shame (Rose & Miller, 2010). This "depoliticization" of social issues is of course highly political, even though the formulas used to describe it are words like evidence-based, objectivity, responsibility, and freedom of choice. By describing it in such self-evident terms rather than ideology, it becomes the only possible attitude in politics, while alternative ideologies are excluded as being non-rational and perhaps even unreasonable.

The field of education for sustainable development—at the research level, the policy level, and in teaching material, as shown in the

---

[6]I must remind readers that this is a text-based study. Soneryd and Uggla (2015) problematize the way in which this obvious steering toward consumption as the important political action really gets people to comply, or if the idea of green citizenship is renegotiated in practice.

examples above and below—has found itself in the middle of this post-political rationality, probably without intending to be there. In recent years, however, this has been observed in several studies.[7] These indicate that the neoliberal understanding of sustainable development means that conflicts are concealed and the questions—which are highly political in nature—are depoliticized with the aid of references to individual consumer choices, technological solutions, or ostensibly objective mathematical calculations (cf. Hertzberg, 2015). Or as Hursh et al. put it:

> In short, neoliberalism seeks to transform environmental issues into economic ones, stripping them of other possible senses and ways of thinking and acting in response to them. The environment, when conceptualized as a commodity, can be assessed in terms of its monetary and exchange value (no matter how we might hesitate over such notions as "natural capital"). Environmental issues and crises are turned into opportunities for entrepreneurialism and technological innovation, rather than a systematic political and cultural rethinking and reworking of our relationships with the environment, including our fellow earthbound inhabitants, human, and otherwise. (Hursh et al., 2015, p. 308)

The focus on knowledge, rationality, and/or individual choice eliminates questions of power, justice, and equality. This renders invisible the central role played by politics and ideology in matters of sustainable development.

Naomi Klein (2015) warns that politics, economics, and environment have been disconnected in the public debate (and definitely in school, according to my analysis). The unwillingness of the big companies and the inability of politicians to regulate are described in frightening detail. On the other hand, Klein also sees solutions through a global redistribution of economic resources. According to the established

---

[7]See e.g. Bengtsson and Östman (2013), Cachelin, Rose, and Paisley (2015), Hasslöf (2015), Ideland and Malmberg (2015), Knutsson (2013), Kopnina (2012), McKenzie (2012), Sund and Öhman (2014), Van Poeck and Östman (2017), Van Poeck, Goeminne, and Vandenabeele (2016).

principle of "the polluter pays," one can claim that the countries that have caused climate change, that is to say, the countries that have had high emissions of carbon dioxide, should also pay for the effects. From this point of view, the climate crisis becomes a possible catalyst to rectify global injustices on many levels—environmental but also economic. Klein obviously considers other perspectives on the politics of the climate issue—the book is a 576-page odyssey about this. And with the aid of this alternative narrative, the focus is shifted from the individual's knowledge and consumption to the game of political and economic power that is being played and the problems caused by the philosophy of growth that pervades today's economic system.

For this outlook to become possible for school children as well, the focus has to fall on difficult political questions and serious conflicts—the global redistribution of economic resources is a trickier topic than switching off the light when you leave the room. The question then must be addressed as political, which often means inconvenient, and virtually impossible to handle in school, which is supposed to deliver politically independent teaching (Hasslöf, 2015). But it is one possible method to capture complexities rather than things that are obvious. Moreover, it can be an opportunity to actually address distinct environmental problems. Helen Kopnina (2012) argues that ESD—with a focus on social and economic development and with a pluralistic approach to it—ignores that there actually are serious environmental problems that must be tackled in school. The anthropocentric perspective conceals the significance of relations between different species.

In view of the fear of conflict and of challenging economic and political power structures, it is presumably no coincidence that it is the environmental organizations the WWF, the Swedish Society for Nature Conservation, and Keep Sweden Clean that are engaging—and being engaged—in Swedish schools. One organization that is missing from the educational context, and one that does not produce any teaching material adapted for school,[8] is Greenpeace, which has anything but a

---

[8]I have searched without success for teaching material on both the Swedish Greenpeace website (http://www.greenpeace.org/sweden/se) and the international site (http://www.greenpeace.org).

post-political approach to environmental issues. Instead of focusing on the need for people to make environmentally friendly consumer choices, they blockade oil rigs and nuclear power plants and they circulate petitions and political appeals. In recent years they have produced and shown advertising films against Shell the oil company, partly by showing an Arctic Lego landscape, with animals and people, being drowned in oil to a version of the song "Everything is Awesome" from the latest Lego film (Greenpeace, 2014).[9] The reason for the film was that Lego wanted to renew its energy agreement with Shell, which they actually did not do after the campaign and the ensuing debate. This Lego film was probably not intended for children but for adults. The message is not nicely wrapped, and it appeals not to the consumer but to the political subject. The concluding sentence, "Shell is polluting our kids' imagination," is followed, not by the words "Stop buying Lego" or "Choose something else," but by the exhortation: "Sign the petition." Greenpeace is a political, activist environmental movement, unlike the WWF, the Swedish Society for Nature Conservation, and Keep Sweden Clean. This means that they are disqualified from school because they can be dismissed as "political" (even if they claim to be independent) or even fundamentalist—and hence not credible. "Political" organizations have no place in the post-political project. Here it is rationality, in combination with optimism, that counts.

References

Ahmed, S. (2004). Affective economies. *Social Text, 22*(2), 117–139.

Ahmed, S. (2010). *The promise of happiness.* Durham: Duke University Press.

Ahmed, S. (2012). *On being included: Racism and diversity in institutional life.* Durham and London: Duke University Press.

Ahmed, S. (2014a). *The cultural politics of emotion* (2nd ed.). Edinburgh: Edinburgh University Press.

---

[9]The title of the Greenpeace film is "LEGO: Everything is NOT awesome," alluding to the song "Everything is Awesome" from *The LEGO Movie* from 2014. The characters of Emmet and Lucy from the original film can also be glimpsed in the Greenpeace film.

Ahmed, S. (2014b). The politics of good feeling. *Critical Race and Whiteness Studies, 10*(2), 1–19.

Anderson, B. (2006). *Imagined communities: Reflections on the origin and spread of nationalism.* Brooklyn: Verso Books.

Andrée, M., Hansson, L., & Ideland, M. (2018). Political agendas and actors in science teaching: An analysis of teaching materials from NGOs and private companies. In A. Arvola-Orlander, K. Othrell-Cass, & M. K. Sillasen (Eds.), *Cultural, social, and political perspectives in science education* (pp. 75–92). Cham: Springer.

Bengtsson, S., & Östman, L. (2013). Globalisation and education for sustainable development: Emancipation from context and meaning. *Environmental Education Research, 19*(4), 477–498.

Bennett, J. (2001). *The enchantment of modern life: Attachments, crossings, and ethics.* Princeton, NJ: Princeton University Press.

Bernstein, B. (2001). From pedagogies to knowledge. In A. Morals, I. Neves, B. Davies, & H. Daniels (Eds.), *Towards a sociology of pedagogy: The contribution of Basil Bernstein to research.* New York: Peter Lang.

Bourdieu, P. (1986). The forms of capital. In I. Szeman & T. Kaposy (Eds.), *Cultural theory: An anthology* (pp. 81–93). Chichester: Blackwell.

Bowden, R. (2005). *Hållbar utveckling: Hotet mot miljön.* Stockholm: Liber.

Cachelin, A., Rose, J., & Paisley, K. (2015). Disrupting neoliberal discourse in critical sustainability education: A qualitative analysis of intentional language framing. *Environmental Education Research, 21*(8), 1127–1142.

Child, L. (2008). *Hjälp vår jord.* Stockholm: Rabén & Sjögren.

Cooke, A. N., Fielding, K. S., & Louis, W. R. (2016). Environmentally active people: The role of autonomy, relatedness, competence and self-determined motivation. *Environmental Education Research, 22*(5), 631–657.

Cowen, R. (2014). With the exception of Switzerland … thoughts about the nation and educational research. *IJHE Bildungsgeschichte 4*(2), 216–228.

Foucault, M. (1983). The subject and power. In H. Dreyfus & P. Rabinow (Eds.), *Michel Foucault: Beyond structuralism and hermeneutics* (pp. 208–226). Chicago, IL: University of Chicago Press.

Foucault, M., Ewald, F., & Fontana, A. (2010). *The birth of biopolitics: Lectures at the Collège de France, 1978–1979* (M. Senellart, Ed.). New York: Palgrave Macmillan.

Gore, A. (2006). *An inconvenient truth.* Paramount Pictures.

Gorur, R. (2014). Towards a sociology of measurement in education policy. *European Educational Research Journal, 13*(1), 58–72.

Gottlieb, D., Vigoda-Gadot, E., & Haim, A. (2013). Encouraging ecological behaviors among students by using the ecological footprint as an educational tool: A quasi-experimental design in a public high school in the city of Haifa. *Environmental Education Research, 19*(6), 844–863.

Greenpeace. (2014). *LEGO: Everything is NOT awesome.* Retrieved April 7, 2016, from https://www.youtube.com/watch?v=qhbliUq0_r4.

Grek, S. (2009). Governing by numbers: The PISA 'effect' in Europe. *Journal of Education Policy, 24*(1), 23–37.

Haraway, D. J. (2016). *Staying with the trouble: Making kin in the Chthulucene.* Durham: Duke University Press.

Hasslöf, H. (2015). *The educational challenge in "education for sustainable development": Qualification, social change and the political.* Malmö: Malmö University. Diss.

Hertzberg, F. (2015). Double gestures of inclusion and exclusion: Notions of learning outcomes, autonomy, and informed choices in Swedish educational and vocational guidance. *International Journal of Qualitative Studies in Education, 28*(10), 1203–1228.

Heyck, H. (2012). Producing reason. In M. Solovey & H. Cravens (Eds.), *Cold war social science: Knowledge production, liberal democracy, and human nature* (pp. 99–116). New York: Palgrave Macmillan.

Hillbur, P., Ideland, M., & Malmberg, C. (2016). Response and responsibility: Fabrication of the eco-certified citizen in Swedish curricula 1962–2011. *Journal of Curriculum Studies, 48*(3), 409–426.

Holmberg, T., & Ideland, M. (2016). Imagination laboratory: Making sense of bio-objects in contemporary genetic art. *Sociological Review, 64*(3), 447–467.

Höhler, S. (2015). *Spaceship earth in the environmental age, 1960–1990.* London: Pickering & Chatto.

Hursh, D., Henderson, J., & Greenwood, D. (2015). Environmental education in a neoliberal climate. *Environmental Education Research, 21*(3), 299–318.

Ideland, M. (2014). How PISA becomes transformed into a Nationalistic Project: Reflections upon a Swedish 'school crisis'. *IJHE Bildungsgeschichte, 4*(2), 243–245.

Ideland, M., & Malmberg, C. (2015). Governing 'eco-certified children' through pastoral power: Critical perspectives on education for sustainable development. *Environmental Education Research, 21*(2), 173–182.

Kampmann, J. (2004a). Det selv-i-agt-tagelige barn. *Psyke & Logos, 25*(2), 21.

Kampmann, J. (2004b). Societalization of childhood: New opportunities? New demands? In H. Brembeck, B. Johansson, & J. Kampmann (Eds.), *Beyond the competent child: Exploring contemporary childhoods in the Nordic welfare societies* (pp. 127–152). Fredriksberg: Roskilde University Press.

Klein, N. (2015). *This changes everything: Capitalism vs. the climate*. New York: Simon & Schuster.

Knutsson, B. (2013). Swedish environmental and sustainability education research in the era of post-politics? *Utbildning & Demokrati 22*(2), 105–122.

Kopnina, H. (2012). Education for sustainable development (ESD): The turn away from 'environment'in environmental education? *Environmental Education Research, 18*(5), 699–717.

Lazzarato, M. (2010). Pastoral power: Beyond public and private. *Open, 19,* 18–32.

Lin, S. M. (2016). Reducing students' carbon footprints using personal carbon footprint management system based on environmental behavioural theory and persuasive technology. *Environmental Education Research, 22*(5), 658–682.

McKenzie, M. (2012). Education for y'all: Global neoliberalism and the case for a politics of scale in sustainability education policy. *Policy Futures in Education, 10*(2), 165–177.

Miller, P. (2004). Governing by numbers: Why calculative practices matter. In A. Amin & N. Thrift (Eds.), *The Blackwell cultural economy reader*. Oxford: Blackwell.

Miller, P., & Rose, N. (2008). *Governing the present*. Cambridge: Polity Press.

Mouffe, C. (2011). *On the political*. Abingdon: Routledge.

Persson, M., Sjöström, B., & Johnsson, P. (2007). *Klimatsmart: Din guide till en miljövänligare vardag*. Stockholm: Alfabeta.

Popkewitz, T. (2011). PISA. In M. A. Pereyra, H. G. Kotthoff, & R. Cowen (Eds.), *PISA under examination: Changing knowledge, changing tests, and changing schools*. Rotterdam: Sense Publishers.

Rizvi, F., & Lingard, B. (2010). *Globalizing education policy*. London: Routledge.

Rose, N. (1991). Governing by numbers: Figuring out democracy. *Accounting, Organizations and Society, 16*(7), 673–692.

Rose, N. (1998). *Inventing our selves: Psychology, power, and personhood*. Cambridge: Cambridge University Press.

Rose, N., & Miller, P. (2010). Political power beyond the state: Problematics of government. *The British Journal of Sociology, 61,* 271–303.

Sellar, S. (2015). A feel for numbers: Affect, data and education policy. *Critical Studies in Education, 56*(1), 131–146.

Simons, M., & Masschelein, J. (2008). The governmentalization of learning and the assemblage of a learning apparatus. *Educational Theory, 58*(4), 391–415.

Soneryd, L., & Uggla, Y. (2015). Green governmentality and responsibilization: New forms of governance and responses to 'consumer responsibility'.
Environmental Politics, 24(6), 913–931.

Sund, l., & Öhman, J. (2014). On the need to repoliticise environmental and sustainability education: Rethinking the postpolitical consensus.
Environmental Education Research, 20, 639–659.

Svenskt näringsliv. (2010). *Miljö – så funkar det.* Stockholm: Svenskt näringsliv.

Typhina, E. (2017). Urban park design + love for nature: Interventions for visitor experiences and social networking. *Environmental Education Research,
23*(8), 1169–1181.

Van Poeck, K., Goeminne, G., & Vandenabeele, J. (2016). Revisiting the democratic paradox of environmental and sustainability education: Sustainability
issues as matters of concern. *Environmental Education Research, 22*(6), 806–826.

Van Poeck, K., & Östman, L. (2017). Creating space for 'the political' in environmental and sustainability education practice: A political move analysis of
educators' actions. *Environmental Education Research*, 1–18. https://doi.org/
10.1080/13504622.2017.1306835.

Weber, M. (2009). *From Max Weber: Essays in sociology.* Abingdon: Routledge.

Witoszek, N. (2018). Teaching sustainability in Norway, China and Ghana:
Challenges to the UN programme. *Environmental Education Research,
24*(6), 831–844.

3

Eco-Certified Energy

Abstract The chapter unpacks how the figuration of the eco-certified child is (re)produced inside a cultural politics of emotions and how the "right" knowledge and actions are thought of as optimizing students' emotions. Through education and activation, students are supposed to engage in the world with a good mood—which makes Environmental and Sustainability Education (ESE) into a "nice" practice avoiding complex problems as well as anger, despair or apathy. These emotions are instead attached to the Other; the one who needs to change to become a desirable citizen. The chapter discusses what this categorization of emotions means in terms of cultural constructions of We and the Other and how the cultural politics of ESE is (re)producing a colonial understanding of the world and its inhabitants.

Keywords Education · Activism · The Other

Extract from the column "ASK SOMETHING ABOUT ENERGY USE!"

Hi,
Often I can't be bothered to do things, such as cleaning my room. Then I get a scolding for that. What should I do?
"Soffan"

Hi Soffan,
Many people think that you have an annoying attitude, but honestly, wouldn't it be great if your attitude had been more common in the human race? Just think if everyone that was involved in, say, the construction of the atom bomb had followed your line and had said, "But quite frankly—who would be bothered splitting uranium, managing a dead-complicated chemical chain reaction, fiddling about in some boring lab, no way, you only live once, let's go back to my place and have some ice cream instead!"
So stick your ground and good luck in the future!

This invented, and ironic, question-and-answer column is quoted from the teaching material published by the Swedish Society for Nature Conservation, *Energifallet* ("The Energy Case," Naturskyddsföreningen, 2013). Besides the question from "Soffan" there are questions from a sun that feels forgotten, a fish stick that thinks it has to travel round the world too much, and a person using the pen name "Worried" who thinks that today's adults behave strangely:

> They just run up and down out of subway stations and into and out of cars on the way to some job, build factories, move them to China, import apples from New Zealand, and start some armed conflict as soon as you turn your back.

A suggestion from the column is that adults need limits and should only be allowed to use fossil fuels on Saturdays... Subtle humor is thus used to highlight different aspects of the energy question. On the front cover of the same issue we see the glaring heading "You are full of energy!" illustrated by a girl with her hair standing straight up because of static electricity. The publication, which is aimed at teachers and pupils in compulsory school, deals with energy in a great many

different ways, both explaining and instructing, as regards body energy
and electricity. But the heading "You are full of energy!" has an addi-
tional meaning: it urges pupils to use their inherent strength to ensure
sustainable development. Their energy too needs to be—figura-
tively speaking—eco-certified. The question is what the demands for
this environmentally friendly (renewable!) energy are like compared
with the "fossil" variant, the antiquated person who does not take personal responsibility or act in accordance with scientific rationality. Can
an eco-certified child really be like "Soffan" in Granér's column—who
"can't be bothered to do things"? Can he or she be passive, inactive, not
bothered? Or should children be "worried" and feel concern about the
adults' environmentally dangerous behavior? These questions are obviously rhetorical, and we all know the answer: the eco-certified child's
environmentally certified energy is utilized to feel responsibility for the
environment, to get involved and take action.

This chapter illuminates and discusses how engagement in environment is made into something that feels self-evident and how good
intentions to engage and activate children and adults contribute to
the (re)production of the division into those who fit in and those who
need to change their ways. Among other ways, this is done by reasoning about why it is better to be active than passive, and what emotions it is "permissible" (discursively possible) to feel and express in
relation to today's environmental problems and visions of the future.
To help me to understand this I have Sara Ahmed (2014) and others
who problematize the cultural politics of emotions: how talk of feelings
conjures up boundaries between imagined community and exclusion.
Ahmed describes, for example, how the nation as an imagined community comes into existence through the talk of a shared shame about
the nation's injustices—a shame that is everyone's and no one's at the
same time. Similarly, talk of fears and commitment is a way to arrive at
a community in the sustainability discourse, in the common project of
saving the world. But this also means that other (or unfelt) emotions,
and (non-)actions define those who are on the outside, those who are
not yet included in the community. Once again, we see the double
gesture of inclusion and exclusion. By holding up certain actions and
emotions as "correct" or perhaps "optimal," others are (re)produced as

wrong—and so are the categories of people that are, at least considered as, expressing the wrong emotions.

The Empowered, Competent Child

In the last chapter, it was claimed that pastoral power operates as a governing technology in ESE. Typical for pastoral power technologies is that they target the soul. The willingness to act must come from the will, from the interior of the mind. The governing of the soul in ESE is particularly done by emphasizing emotions. Erica Burman (2009) claims that education in general has gone through an "emotional turn." Feelings and affects—emotional literacy—have lately been given a prominent place in the general educational culture. Even beyond the hegemonic psychological discourse claiming the importance of internal motivation and other psychological understandings of education, we can talk about a therapeutic culture in which emotions are seen as needed for learning, and for changing the subject. We can particularly see this in recent research about ESE that studies the relation between emotions and learning in different ways (e.g. Andersson, 2018; Håkansson, Östman, & Van Poeck, 2018; Manni, Sporre, & Ottander, 2017). To learn—that is to say, to change to a more sustainable understanding of the world—requires that you actually feel something, that you are "struck and shaken" in your soul and thus become willing to do things (Bennett, 2001, p. 4).

As an example of a way to teach in order to change individuals radically, we can take a look at a specific practice in ESE: teaching for action competence.[1] The intention of this practice is to help children and youngsters develop:

> an ability, on the basis of critical thinking and an incomplete knowledge base, to engage as a person and with others in responsible actions and counteractions for a more humane and merciful world. (Almers, 2009, p. 36)

---

[1] For a deeper analysis of the practice and ideas behind teaching action-competence see Ideland (2016).

At the core of teaching action competence lies the aim to foster "action-minded citizens" (Breiting, Hedegaard, Mogensen, Nielsen, & Schnack, 2009), individuals willing and able to engage in environmental problems and who can contribute to social change now and in the future. The pedagogical idea of teaching for action competence was developed in the 1980–1990s, in the MUVIN program. MUVIN is an acronym for "Miljöundervisning i Norden" (Environmental Education in the Nordic Countries). When it started to develop as a pedagogical practice it was described as a "new paradigm in environmental education" (Breiting et al., 2009, p. 16). Its epistemological roots are connected to German critical theory and the American sociologist C. Wright Mills's concept of sociological imagination. The main idea is to work with "visions for the future" (ibid., p. 17) rather than trying to convince students of how to live their lives in the present. In the late 1980s, the novelty of action competence was thus to develop students' skills for handling environmental issues and to prepare them for an uncertain future (Breiting et al., 2009, p. 56), or wicked problems, that will say dilemmas so complex that there might not exist a solution, only different ways to handle them (Lotz-Sisitka, Wals, Kronlid, & McGarry, 2015; Rittel & Webber, 1973). Hence, the target for ESE is not the environment in itself; rather, it is the individual and his/her resilience, adaptability, and preparedness to act. However, to become this person, knowledge about the environment must be combined with a certain individual disposition:

> These personality-related aspects are the willingness, courage, and inclination to involve oneself. And this is also a matter of taking responsibility for one's own and others' lives and trusting one's own power of action or influencing possibilities. Hence, action competence is seen as a personal capacity embracing rather more than the intellectual-cognitive domain. It involves the entire personality, including many of the mental performance potentials and dispositions. (Breiting et al., 2009, p. 50)

Willingness and courage are thus typical feelings that label the eco-certified person. Other markers that stick to this figuration are engagement, self-confidence, and empowerment. The sense of empowerment is a feeling that you are playing a part in handling the problem, and doing your bit. It also involves that your voice is being heard and that you are significant. This discourse is materialized in most of the teaching material studied, and can be expressed as in a teaching material from the WWF targeting preschool pedagogy:

> When children feel that they have the right to exert influence, their self-esteem is strengthened. Children's influence can take different forms:
> - responsibility for composting
> - sorting waste
> - flushing toilets
> - light managers who ensure that no lights are left on when the preschool closes
>
> (WWF, 2012, p. 9)

We recognize the activities from the previous chapter. In this discourse the child is not the opposite of an adult but an equal, sufficiently competent to participate in society—and children must therefore be given opportunities to assume responsibility for society—even if they are only three or four years old. This responsibility must be understood in a specific historical context, with a specific outlook on childhood as children as miniature version of adults, rather than significantly different from them (Ideland, 2016; Nadesan, 2010). In this pedagogical discourse, the idea of the child as the unfinished citizen is obvious, who should develop specific traits and skills—and emotions—to become a responsible adult. Since the 1990s the figuration of "the competent child" has a prominent position in educational discourses, producing a rupture in the view of the child. Children are made up as equal to adults and competent enough to participate in society—human beings rather than human becomings (Ellergard, 2004, p. 178). Brembeck et al. state that since the 1990s:

> A new understanding of the child has been presented: that of a social and cultural being, an adequate member of society, who acts, reflects and contributes to its own growth as well as the growth of society. Children are attributed agency, and constructions of subjectivities are understood as ongoing processes where identities are negotiated. (Brembeck, Johansson, & Kampmann, 2004, p. 18)

Historically, in educational discourses, the child is transformed from being subjected to teachability and developmentality to being subjected to accountability and sociability; now it is a reliable child, who is worth listening to (Brembeck et al., 2004; Hultqvist & Dahlberg, 2001). A little bit surprisingly, the child is constructed as even more responsible and reasonable than adults, instead of being an imperfect (unfinished) adult. I would claim that this is particularly noticeable in the discourse of ESE, which constructs the child as an environmental agent, the present as well as the future citizen. The young child is not yet contaminated by cynicism and capitalism but as a "pure soul," plastic in his/her identity and also more close to the nature that s/he is expected to protect (Ärlemalm-Hagsér, 2013).

Learning to Will Right

The book *Beyond the Competent Child* also analyzes which children are constructed as competent and which are defined as incompetent—the undesirable child, the future citizen who will not contribute to the development of society. Embedded in good intentions of giving the children agency and empowerment, with the help of Popkewitz (2012) we can observe that in a double gesture there is a—probably involuntary—exclusion of children who are not courageous, engaged, or empowered. The child who, for various reasons, cannot exercise agency or is not "willing" to "do the right thing." A solution to this, of course, is education—a technology of will.[2] Pedagogy and education are ways to foresee that the citizen is/becomes willing in the right way (Ahmed, 2012, p. 7). Sara Ahmed talks about this technology as a virtue of willingness. Again we can relate to Foucault's (1983) theories of pastoral power, how the salvation of the individual is tied to the work for a common good: saving the flock. Ahmed expresses it in similar way:

---

[2]The analysis of willingness and willfulness, happiness duty etc. in ESE is elaborated in Ideland (2017).

The will duty is a reproductive duty: the part must willingly take part, and must participate in the reproduction of the whole. The parts must also aim for the happiness and health of the whole. (Ahmed, 2012, p. 6)

The opposite of willingness might be willfulness—the wrong will—the one that, instead of keeping the flock together, threatens the societal body and the common will. If one puts oneself before the whole, "then one must learn to will right" (Ahmed, 2012, p. 4). Ahmed continues:

A willful part would cause the unhappiness or ill health of the body of which it is a part. The very diagnosis of willfulness provides a moral frame that allows some parts to be read as putting themselves before the whole. (Ahmed, 2012, p. 6)

Through what Ahmed calls "archives of willfulness" such as fairy tales, folklore, fiction, curricula, and moral philosophies, the willful child has throughout history been constructed as the affect alien. This figuration operates as a terrifying example of what happens to children not willing to adapt to the common will. In these—often scary—stories the Other simultaneously operates as a warning of a unwanted behavior and as a strengthening of the cultural theses of how to live and feel. Ahmed (2012) exemplifies willfulness from Grimm's fairy tale, "The Willful Child." This is a story of a child so stubborn that neither her mother, God, nor any doctor could help her, so she got sick and died. However, even from the afterlife, she exerted her own will by repeatedly raising her arm from the grave—until her mother hit it with a rod. Eventually the girl's will was overcome. The problematic individual, the affect alien, in this story was thus not the (from a modern perspective) vicious mother, but the willful child. Undoubtedly, this story is from a time long before discourses of empowered and action-competent children (Ideland, 2016). But today, similar (maybe more political correct) narratives can be found in everything from fiction to scholarly works. In the world of popular culture, it is quite easy to see that stereotypes of the willful subject, unwilling to adapt to the group, are often the same person who gets into trouble. Sometimes even gets killed. The affect alien in the shape of a egoistic, greedy, or simply lazy person, with no interest in the common good, is a dangerous person for society as well as for him/herself. More particularly, in popular culture with an environmental theme, the unwilling person is a recurring character—and the one that needs to change for the salvation of the flock—today and in the future—the next life in pastoral terms. For instance, in the movie *Tomorrowland* (2015), environmental crises can be solved only if mankind are willing to change and believes that it is possible, Unfortunately for the world, there are obstinate, unflexible, willful persons (mostly adults) who are not willing to follow and thus become—quite literally—threats to the world.

The horrible stories of what happens to the willful person, as in Grimm's fairy tale or Hollywood movies, might not be appropriate in the educational discourse of today. A less scary archive of willfulness could be research publications about the dispositions of the successful and unsuccessful students in ESE: the promising citizen versus the student at risk. Speaking with the voice of expertise, these articles can be said to translating cultural theses of willingness, willfulness and proper behaviors into scientific truths (and vice versa) (Rose & Miller, 2010). One apparent example of the targeting of the interior of the mind and the domestication of emotions is found in the work of the Swedish educational psychologist Maria Ojala. She has studied how the students' abilities to mobilize hope of a better future impacts their willingness to engage in climate change and—in the prolonging—their development of action competence (Ojala, 2015). But the hope could not be of any kind. One of Ojala's findings is that hope needs to be based on knowledge to contribute to the development of action competence. Students who had hope for the world for the reason that they felt empowered to make a change through individual actions were—maybe not surprisingly—also willing to engage. On the contrary, students who felt hope because they denied climate change didn't see the point of changing their habits. Some kinds of hope were not treasured, rather categorized as wrong. These willful students became in Ahmed terms a kind of *affect aliens*. Those who felt the right thing, but for the wrong reasons, became positioned on the outside of the community and thus also as objects of inclusion.

In other words, even when it comes to emotions, the idea of normality is including and excluding, and educational practices do not seldom aim to make students' feelings compatible with the cultural theses of the desirable citizen. In this case, certain feelings are culturally elevated, such as engagement, optimism, and empowerment. Their opposites are despair, anxiety, and apathy—feelings that are often considered as non-productive. Studies of teaching for action competence describe these feelings as something to avoid, since they run counter to "the ultimate goal of environmental teaching" (Breiting et al., 2009, p. 33). The feelings must thus be mastered. Living in a therapeutic culture means that emotions must be articulated, but also controlled and administrable (Bartholdsson, 2014). Concepts that flourish in the world of school are emotional intelligence, emotional management, that is, how to deal with one's feelings, and emotional literacy, which means the ability to understand and use feelings (Kenway & Youdell, 2011). Using one's emotions in the right way has become a competence on a par with other literacies; being able to use one's language, one's scientific or mathematical knowledge in different contexts.

On the surface, the focus on emotions seems to contest ideas of objectivity and reason in education. Jane Bennett (2001) even proposes a need for human beings to be enchanted as a way to escape the modern society's perception of rationality, and develop new ethical approaches to the environment. But in line with Erica Burman (2009), I claim that the "emotional cultural turn" in education functions alongside its binary opposite, scientization. In this entanglement of feelings and rationality, some emotions are considered productive for learning, while others are simply disturbing. These feelings are sometimes described as "irrational" (Gagen, 2013), which means that feelings become a part of the rationality discourse that sets its stamp on modernity's belief that the world can be organized and planned.

In the academic literature on ESE there are examples of attempts to combine rationality and emotionality, to show how feelings can become a part of the modern rational project. Ojala's studies of how one can "optimize" pupils' emotions so that anxiety leads to optimism and vigorous action are one example. The rational view of emotions and what they "ought" to be like is striking, as is the faith in the ability of education to domesticate and optimize emotions in the right way.

The Virtue of Happiness

In earlier studies on ESE, the feeling of guilt is pointed out as a governing technology of the self. In the individualization of environmental problems, a pastoral discourse directing the soul is used to knit together personal guilt with global threats, detailed individual activities with possibilities of rescuing the flock and the planet (Ideland & Malmberg, 2015; cf. Foucault, 1983). The expectations of competent children to produce emotions such as compassion and engagement strike back at them and guilt arises if they do not feel adequately compassionate and engaged (Johansson, 2004, p. 234). The discourse of action competence, with intentions to foster students' emotions toward courage and willingness, is supposed to protect the students from guilt. Instead, the eco-certified child is supposed to feel joy and optimism. The picture of happy, active children is common in the Swedish ESE discourse, where happiness and environmental action are combined. This happy child can be compared to the child that the American historian Finis Dunaway (2015) describes in his book exploring the images used in the environmental movement: vulnerable children subjected to environmental threats. In contrast to these objects of fear in one certain kind of environmental discourse, the child in the Swedish educational discourse is constructed as the joyful, empowered child that is going to solve environmental problems rather than suffer from them. They are made up as ready to do as in the commercial slogan mentioned in the last chapter: "Save the world a little every day." The modern Swedish child—in educational settings—feels competent and does things, even if the actions often are symbolic rather than impacting the environment. These engagements may be anything from making collages of recycled trash to collecting cartons or writing letters to people in power. The action, in itself, becomes a marker for the problem-solving child, at least as long as it is done in a positive way. Like the success stories about willing people, the actions in themselves are supposed to be "uplifting." The actions contribute to the displacement of the negative feelings that arise when subjected to looming environmental catastrophes.

Stories and portraits of happy children, as well as articles about how to successfully optimize emotions, operate as archives of happiness, if we continue to speak with Sara Ahmed. Happiness is of course something desirable, which we all strive for. However, as any desirable traits, ideas of happiness construct the Other. Ahmed talks about a "happiness duty" in contemporary culture; to be positive instead of dwelling on negative experiences of racism and power relations. Happiness thus becomes a boundary marker delineating those who deal with societal problems in a reasonable way and those who deal with them in the wrong way, by being angry, furious, and protesting loudly. Emotions make up the boundary between the reasonable and the unreasonable subjectivities by defining the killjoys (Ahmed, 2014). Killjoys are those who do not adapt to the happy language of hope and possibilities. Instead, they disturb the order by their very presence. However, killjoys don't inhabit the Swedish educational discourse on sustainability, environment, and action competence. We can find many examples of how children challenge the adult (environmentally cynical) world, but never by being troublesome or angry. These are best described as a discursive silence, which of course also is important for the construction of the eco-certified child and his/her Other. As noted in the first chapter, discourses organize and condition possible ways to live, talk and feel by what is said but also what remains unsaid.

The outspoken affect alien in the happiness discourse is the one in despair who is not able to engage. In the Swedish discourse, these Others who are described as lacking agency are almost always positioned somewhere else, for example, in the southern and eastern parts of the world (from a European point of view). Stories about these unempowered, non-modern people, always portrayed as objects of help, can be seen as archives of sadness. Through repeated stories of poverty, environmental catastrophes, and nonfunctioning governments in places somewhere else, the fabrication of the empowered child in the North/ West becomes even stronger. These stories are embedded in a traditional, colonial understanding of the world—in which emotions always have been a boundary marker for social categorizations. The reasonable, empowered white Western man is constructed through making the Other, e.g. the woman or the "savage," into the one with uncontrolled, unproductive feelings (McClintock, 1995), such as being in despair.

The archive of sadness is one more technology of emotions, making up a certain kind of citizen as someone whose positive attitude is entangled with an environmentally friendly way of living (which one definitely can question concerning the Swedish children). Other feelings, such as anxiety and "unwell-being," which could make sense in relation to the environmental discourse since doomsday stories are quite frequent, are thus projected onto the affect alien. Emotions make up the borders for the saviors and those needing to be saved in a double gesture of inclusion and exclusion: the competent, active problem-solver versus the passive (in the sense of unable as well as unwilling) problem to be solved. From this point of view, the focus on emotions in the work for a more sustainable and just world thus risks contributing to the establishment of an unjust social order rather than a common future for all.

Protection Through Activation

I can vividly imagine, nevertheless, how environmental issues and apocalyptic narratives of climate catastrophes, extinct species, and waste mountains could cause anxiety in children as in adults. Guilt too. At least they regularly do that to me. The protection against these unwelcome and unproductive emotions is—once again—to "do things." An example (far too long, but telling) comes from Stellan Sandh, CEO of the educational publisher Svenska Kunskapsförlaget, on the subject of their publication of *Natur- och Miljöboken* ("The Nature and Environment Book"):

Every year, the "new words" of the year are published. These words enter dictionaries while other, outdated words disappear. In 2007, the term "climate anxiety" was published with the definition "anxiety about a threatening climate deterioration." [...] Of course, it is not only climate anxiety that fills our lives—other expressions turn up [in the Swedish language], such as "entourage" ("companions to a VIP") and "pimping" ("making more luxurious"), among others—glitter terms about dubious dreams of success. [...]

As far as I know, there is no specific psychotherapy for worries concerning environmental degradation. We have to take care of that in another way—by hand—such as living more environmentally friendly. It is a task for us all. [...] It is then that we need to think about how our small gestures are more important than we think. [...]

The letter materializes how ESE operates as a promise of happiness and how this can be achieved by *doing* things: "Small gestures are more important than we think," as stated in the email. In this discourse, children's fears for an unsustainable future can, and should, be transformed into hope and happiness through practical work.

Speaking more theoretically, this way of making bad feelings go away by doing things can be understood through what Miller and Rose (2008) call the principles of activation and responsibilization. In the advanced liberal society these are crucial since the will and the actions of the free individual must find a way to fit into the will of the nation. The individual becomes personally responsible for the security of the state— or in the case of sustainability and environment: the world. Everyone needs to "do something," even if it is small gestures (activation), for the common good (responsibilization) (see also Ideland, 2016). The boundaries between the public and the private, the national and the individual, and the social and the personal become discursively erased (Miller & Rose, 2008; Popkewitz, 2004). For instance, in the environmental discourse the relation between the actions of individuals (e.g. buying organic food and recycling) and global ecological sustainability is repeatedly emphasized. This feeling of being personally responsible for the common good is inscribed in individuals' souls through different technologies governing how to be, feel, and act as a conscientious person (cf. Foucault, Senellart, & Davidson, 2007).

As Popkewitz (2012) describes this, people's souls are "cleansed" of sin with the aid of democratic actions in the educational system. One can arrange garbage-picking days, appoint children who make sure that lights are switched off, or involve them in a composting project. Through this one can help the children to display the right emotions, to organize them so that worry and anxiety are transformed into more productive feelings such as self-confidence and joy, if we may believe the genre of pictures typically found in teaching material about environment and sustainability. Work for sustainable development becomes a promise of genuine happiness (Ahmed, 2010), beyond the "glittery" happiness based on pimping and entourage as in the quotation above. It feels good to work for sustainability and the environment. In other words, one way to view it is that the self is in focus, even when it is a matter of charity. In the same way, in the introduction I let Wendy Brown point out that the self is strengthened by the feeling of being tolerant. Feeling good, with the conviction that one's actions are good, is important in the construction of the eco-certified person. In particular, this also reflects what Ahmed (2010) writes about the white middle-class idea that what feels good must also be good.

Real, Rational Actions

But it is not just any actions that feel good. In order to identify which actions one should or should not use one's eco-certified energy for, I have examined texts about educating children in action competence, since the authors of these texts give clear definitions of which actions count, and which are just "activities"—that is to say, things that do not mean so much. Precisely this distinction is interesting in the analysis of the eco-certified child since it makes it clear that the question of "how one should live" has rather little to do with actual environmental effects and quite a lot to do with identity construction. For the sake of "Nature" or "the Planet," the intention behind the action, the degree of engagement or genuineness, scarcely has any significance. Researchers in the field of teaching for action competence are fully aware of this, and their wish that education will change people (not the world) is explicit (Breiting et al., 2009). But once again I need to remind you as a reader that the desire to include people in a specific practice also entails powerful excluding forces. The definition of the person who does the things for the right reason also creates the Other, although what this person does (or does not do) may sometimes be even more significant for the environment. It is more a matter of how people "are" and "think" than the actual environmental result.

The first criterion if an action is to "count" as sustainable is the *intentionality*. Actions must be "conscious, reflected, and targeted. [...]

Actions are intentional" (Breiting et al., 2009, p. 44). Actions do not just simply happen. They are the result of careful consideration and planning and should be defendable through logical reasoning. Sorting garbage, for instance, can be counted as an activity if unintentional, but as an action if it is reflected on. The action-competent student is not only active and vigorous, but also self-managed and knowledgeable (cf. Breiting et al., 2005). The actions should be motivated and legitimated by knowledge of why and how. In the Swedish curricula there is a strong link between knowledge, choices, and actions. This particularly applies in relation to the science subjects in school. The learning goals clearly specify that science subjects should be used in the work for sustainability:

> The teaching shall give the pupils opportunities to use and develop knowledge and tools to formulate arguments of their own and scrutinize others' arguments in contexts where a knowledge of chemistry is significant. This will give the pupils what they need to handle practical, ethical, and aesthetic choices concerning energy, the environment, health, and society. (Skolverket, 2011, p. 144)

Despite the reluctance to point out exactly what knowledge will solve what problems, there is a strong belief that knowledge of the natural sciences is useful—or even indispensable. The eco-certified child is thus the knowledgeable, aware child. The Other thus becomes the spontaneous, nonreflective, unknowing child—the childish child. This also answers to other aspects of childhood in what is usually referred to as the knowledge society. In this cultural setting not only perceived societal problems but also childhood in itself is educationalized. Children are expected to engage in learning, not only in school but also in leisure time, fabricating subjectivities constantly able to use knowledge, and to be observant of learning possibilities.

Other criteria for the required way to take action are *authenticity* and that the students *participate genuinely* (Breiting et al., 2005, p. 30). The action-competent child works with authentic problems, solved in authentic ways, resulting in authentic experiences. The opposite is traditional (abstract and theoretical) schooling, with made-up problems, solved for the sake of the teacher, resulting in teaching and learning for tests and grades (Jensen & Schnack, 2006, p. 484). The subjects fitting into this discourse are seen as only responsible for themselves and not for the world. The literature on action competence is filled with examples of teachers' practical work with authentic projects that oblige genuine participation from the students (Björneloo, 2012; Breiting et al., 2009).

In other words, sorting waste by force of habit or because someone has made you do so is not an action that counts in education for competent action (or in society as a whole?). But if you sort waste because you want to save natural resources and/or reduce the waste mountain, and if in addition you have knowledge about sorting and its consequences, the action counts and contributes to your identity as a competent and environmentally friendly person. What we have here is a materialization of the cultural thesis of cosmopolitanism: "by (re) visioning Enlightenment hopes about reason and rationality through an agency directed to ordering the present and the future" (Popkewitz, 2009: 258).

Let me give examples of this culture of doing and what it means. *Mofflor och människor* ("Moffles and People"), which is a teaching material aimed at preschool, describes do-it-yourself projects, experiments with decomposition, producing toys, making paper, collage using rubbish, and many, many other creative ideas. All this comes under the heading "To do." Similar hints aimed at adults outside school can be found, for example, in the book *Klimatsmart: Din guide till en miljövänligare vardag* ("Climate-smart: Your Guide to a More Environment-Friendly Life," Persson, Sjöström, & Johnsson, 2007). The 150 pages in this book are full of facts of the type "Did you know that …?" and "What happens when …?," alternating with "10 simple tips for climate-smarter homes," "8 tips for the workplace," and so on. In this culture of doing, the manufacture of a collage of waste is as significant for the environment as eating only vegetarian food or taking the train instead of flying. The main thing is that you *do something*, in an engaged and determined manner. The tips function as governing technologies to normalize the individual's responsibility and actions. There is nothing wrong with this—and perhaps it is difficult to envisage alternative ways to work with environmental issues with small children. But one may wonder about the story that is not told. If work for sustainability is equated with the individual's activity, the focus is moved from structural injustices and problems. The culture of doing, which was discussed in the last chapter, is yet another piece in the puzzle in the individualization of the environmental issue.

The actions also have a performative function, in that the eco-certified person comes into existence by public display of his or her actions—not just doing them in the home where nobody sees them. A few years ago there was a statement circulating in the environmental debate (I have not been able to establish whether it is true or not), to the effect that consumers bought more ecological food in shops where the ecological products were visible in the trolley than if they bought food online, where no one but the consumer can see the contents of the digital trolley. Whether the statement is correct or not, it (re)produces the notion that it is important to display one's environmental commitment. Interest organizations often offer people the chance to do such performative actions. As described above, one can make climate pledges online. On the websites of environmental organizations such as Keep Sweden Clean one can upload pictures from the school class's battery hunt via Instagram (iconosquare.com/tag/batterijakten) and on the website of the Swedish Society for Nature Conservation you can upload the class's "energy book" (energiboken.naturskyddsforeningen. se). Naturally, this is also intended to make the pupils' work visible and thus inspire others. But another way to view it is that the good performative action becomes a part of the individual's or the school class's identity production. Environmental consciousness is then regarded as a symbolic capital that is invested in the production of a class identity, an imagined community with kindred spirits (Bourdieu, 1986). To be honest, it does feel good, even for adults, to show off one's eco-labels, whether on wine bottles, food, clothes, electronic devices, or cars—in real life as on social media, at least in contexts where the discourse, the truth, about the environmentally friendly life organizes our existence— which is also the very point of the comparison with symbolic capital. Ecological capital is a currency that is valid in certain situations but not in others. This is particularly true in the culture of the educated middle class, where the knowledgeable and conscious person, with the ability and the opportunity, is rewarded.

Once again, one can reflect on the lack of discussion about issues such as who actually does/consumes "too much" and "unnecessarily" and what it means to be passive instead of action-competent. Passivity, nonaction, can be just as environmentally friendly, and perhaps we should sometimes try to teach passive competence to children in school. But passivity does not serve to create identity in the same way because it is not visible (being seen often requires action). In the world of school there are no rewards at all for non-doing; here governing technologies such as public energy books, do-it-yourself projects, and energy surveys in the home (re)produce people who *do* things and who make good use of their eco-certified, hopefully renewable, energy. The undesirable subject—the Other—who must change in order to become an action-competent person, is someone who is unwilling or, for various reasons, unable to act. The educational material also presupposes an "ordinary child" who lives a life in which it is no problem to bring along things like tins, marmalade jars, and bottles to school. Sometimes the child is even assumed to have access to a garden where it is possible to compost things, and a forest where they can play and acquire a positive attitude to nature. The child is moreover presumed to have language that is functional enough to write letters to politicians, and toys that can be given away because they are "superfluous" or they have "tired" of them. It is never articulated in the texts that children might have different possibilities and circumstances. In the name of good intentions, everyone is to be included in the practice. As we have seen, it is humankind as a homogeneous group that is the focus of the project for sustainable development, and it seems virtually impossible to talk of class differences in this context.

Eco-Certified Emotions

Being an eco-certified person also means being able to express emotions; the right feelings in the right situation. The eco-certified person is energetic—full of energy, but with highly specific kinds of energy. As we shall see below, examples of "approved" emotions in the sustainability discourse are self-confidence, a willingness to change, and empowerment, whereas anger, resignation, and passivity are culturally unsuitable. Borrowing terms from Sara Ahmed (2014), one could say that the figuration of the eco-certified child is (re)produced through a cultural economy of emotions. With the aid of economic metaphors, Ahmed shows how emotions function as capital that circulates and accumulates value. Some emotions are valid currency, while others are viewed as being more or less worthless in a specific context. With this outlook, emotions, which are usually regarded as individual and even intimate, can be seen as socially organized, and they organize which capital one can invest in order to be considered a desirable person.[3] As Ahmed describes, it, emotions glue communities, simultaneously creating boundaries and excluding people. As certain emotions stick to certain bodies, their value also accumulates in the emotional economy. If the term "environmentally committed" sticks to a white middle-class body, while the word "hopelessness" simultaneously sticks to a brown or black refugee's body, the different value of these emotions accumulates when the discourse is (re)produced. On the other hand, "environmentally committed" is a term that sticks to a highly specific form of environmental commitment: one of the non-dangerous kind: nonpolitical, non-despairing, non-cursed. The opposites of these qualities stick to the environmental activist, the fundamentalist—an impossible position for the figuration of the eco-certified child, at least in the Swedish ESE discourse. He or she displays instead an independent, positive, and rational attitude. The eco-certified child demands no collective indicatives arising from feelings of hopelessness, repression, or anger at a society that consumes nature's resources. The eco-certified person is organized on the basis of a moderately strong engagement through consumption, waste sorting, and donations to (realistic) voluntary organizations. By displaying and defining what the emotions and actions are supposed to be, the truth about the good, rational, action-competent citizen is constructed.

---

[3]The section on the organization of emotions is likewise based on results and analyses in the article "The Action-Competent Child" (Ideland, 2016) and the book chapter "The End of the World and a Promise of Happiness" (Ideland, 2017).

Of course, the idea of the political activist as the Other is not expressed explicitly; rather, it is created through silences—through an absence of narratives. An amusing and illustrative example of this emotional politics which appears to have become extinct in Swedish environmental teaching is the children's book *Sprätten satt på toaletten* ("Spree sat on the toilet," Elmqvist, 1970/2012). In this story from 1970 a director named Spree builds a factory beside the bay in a town and "nothing has been the same since then … but Spree grew *frightfully* rich." He earned huge amounts of money, but the environment in the bay was destroyed. Children fell ill and the fish died, but Spree thought only about his money, as a true capitalist. The interesting thing is how the people in the town tackled the environmental problem. Did they realize their consumer power and stop buying Spree's products? Or did the children content themselves with cleaning up the bay and feeling how their souls were cleansed? Was it in fact the children who solved the problem, as happens in children's literature, films, and games on environmental themes in the 2010s? No, of course not. The adults became angry and sad, and together they rushed to Spree and took over the factory.

The book about Spree concerns how collective anger and action change society, As opposed to the idea of changed individuals. The focus on emotions in the educational system, and perhaps in other sectors of society, is also part of the general individualization, at the expense of more collective ideals. "The truth," in Foucault's sense, is now that it is individuals, with the right emotions and practical actions, who are agents with the power to change social problems such as pollution, and not political processes or collective efforts. Individuals learn to feel that this is good, since positive emotions have stuck to the major issues of the future and displaced anger and anxiety and other difficult feelings. The focus on self-confidence and individual happiness suits the political landscape today. It was different in the days of Spree in the 1970s, when anger and collective actions were valued and other truths, behaviors, and subjectivities were possible. It is important to point out, however, that I am not trying to spread the message that everything was better in the past. In the environmental movement of the 1970s, of course, people and actions were also (re)produced as problematic or desirable. My point is that there can be other narratives to tell about the environmentally friendly life, narratives that can contain the need for other emotions—anger about injustices and environmental degradation but also passivity and the feeking for not doing things (like consuming, traveling, etc.). Don't get stuck in the single story.

In the definition of this "reasonable" person, the construction of the Other is inescapable. "Reasonable" actions and emotions become indicators of who is included in the community and who is singled out as an object for potential inclusion so that they will not risk endangering either their own position in society or society as a whole (Nadesan, 2010; Popkewitz & Lindblad, 2004, p. 232). Proceeding from the opposite of the desirable person, the Others here are the powerless, cowardly, pessimistic, passive—but also those who are spontaneous and unable to control their emotions. This may seem paradoxical, but the words *passion* and *passivity* have the same origin in the Latin word for suffering, *passio*, and both are regarded as the antithesis of the rational behavior of modernity. Both are also outside the cultural protocol for the eco-certified citizen (Ideland, 2016). When it comes to children, one could say that the undesirable child is childish, with properties that we associate with childhood such as spontaneity and emotionality. But the description here of the undesirable Other also resembles frequently (re) produced notions about, for instance, women, people of color, "fundamentalists," or even "natives"—those who have to be fostered and educated to become more reasonable subjects, steered by logical actions and by organized and productive emotions of self-confidence, optimism, and empowerment[4] (McClintock, 1995; McElhinny, 2010). In other words, I claim that the focus on emotions and actions (re)produces traditional notions of normality and otherness, of gender, nationality, social class and level of education. Moreover, although I have not touched on it here and it is not the major focus of this book, categories of mental health and ill health are constructed. Those who cannot control their emotions, or logically justify their actions, also risk becoming

---

[4]On the other hand, many feminist theorists have tried to upgrade the significance of emotions in society and in research, as part of an emancipation project (besides Bennett, 2001, see Burman, 2009 for further references).

"mentally impaired." Those who display emotions either too much or too little (ADHD or autism) challenge modernity's limits for normality (Börjesson & Palmblad, 2003). These people also become the Other in the sustainability discourse, as the kind of people who threaten the future with their way of living and feeling.

References

Ahmed, S. (2010). *The promise of happiness*. Durham: Duke University Press.

Ahmed, S. (2012). Whiteness and the general will: Diversity work as willful work. *Philosophia, 2*(1), 1–20.

Ahmed, S. (2014). *The cultural politics of emotion* (2nd ed.). Edinburgh: Edinburgh University Press.

Almers, E. (2009). *Handlingskompetens för hållbar utveckling: Tre berättelser om vägen dit*. Jönköping: Högskolan för lärande och kommunikation.

Andersson, P. (2018). Business as un-usual through dislocatory moments— Change for sustainability and scope for subjectivity in classroom practice. *Environmental Education Research, 24*(5), 648–662.

Ärlemalm-Hagsér, E. (2013). *Engagerade i världens bästa? Lärande för hållbarhet i förskolan*. Gothenburg: Gothenburg University. Diss.

Bartholdsson, Å. (2014). Narrating anger: Conceptualisations and representations of children's anger in programmes for social and emotional learning. *Power and Education, 6*(3), 295–306.

Bennett, J. (2001). *The enchantment of modern life: Attachments, crossings, and ethics*. Princeton, NJ: Princeton University Press.

Bird, B. (2015). *Tomorrowland*. Walt Disney Productions.

Björneloo, I. (2012). Handlingskompetens på schemat. In K. Rönnerman (Ed.), *Aktionsforskning i praktiken – förskola och skola på vetenskaplig grund*. Studentlitteratur: Lund.

Börjesson, M., & Palmblad, E. (2003). *I problembarnens tid: Förnuftets moraliska ordning*. Stockholm: Carlssons.

Bourdieu, P. (1986). The forms of capital. In I. Szeman & T. Kaposy (Eds.), *Cultural theory: An anthology* (pp. 81–93). Chichester: Blackwell.

Breiting, S., Mayer, M., & Mogensen, F. (2005). Quality criteria for ESD-schools. *Guidelines to enhance the quality of education for sustainable development*. Vienna: Austrian Federal Ministry of Education, Science, and Culture.

Breiting, S., Hedegaard, K., Mogensen, F., Nielsen, K., & Schnack, K. (2009). *Action competence, conflicting interests and environmental education—The MUVIN Programme*. Odense: Odense Universitetsforlag.

Brembeck, H., Johansson, B., & Kampmann, J. (2004). Introduction. In H. Brembeck, B. Johansson, & J. Kampmann (Eds.), *Beyond the competent child: Exploring contemporary childhoods in the Nordic welfare societies* (pp. 7–32). Fredriksberg: Roskilde University Press.

Burman, E. (2009). Beyond 'emotional literacy' in feminist and educational research. *British Educational Research Journal, 35*(1), 137–155.

Dunaway, F. (2015). *Seeing green: The use and abuse of American environmental images*. Chicago: University of Chicago Press.

Ellergard, T. (2004). Self-governance and incompetence: Teachers' construction of "the competent child". In H. Brembeck, B. Johansson, & J. Kampmann (Eds.), *Beyond the competent child: Exploring contemporary childhoods in the Nordic welfare societies* (pp. 177–198). Fredriksberg: Roskilde University Press.

Elmqvist, A. (1970/2012). *Sprätten satt på toaletten*. Stockholm: Karneval förlag.

Foucault, M. (1983). The subject and power. In H. Dreyfus & P. Rabinow (Eds.), *Michel Foucault: Beyond structuralism and hermeneutics* (pp. 208–226). Chicago, IL: University of Chicago Press.

Foucault, M., Senellart, M., & Davidson, A. I. (2007). *Security, territory, population*. Basingstoke: Palgrave Macmillan.

Gagen, E. A. (2013). Governing emotions: Citizenship, neuroscience and the education of youth. *Transactions of the Institute of British Geographers, 40*, 140–152.

Håkansson, M., Östman, L., & Van Poeck, K. (2018). The political tendency in environmental and sustainability education. *European Educational Research Journal, 17*(1), 91–111.

Hultqvist, K., & Dahlberg, G. (Eds.). (2001). *Governing the child in the new millennium*. Sussex, UK: Psychology Press.

Ideland, M., & Malmberg, C. (2015). Governing 'eco-certified children' through pastoral power: Critical perspectives on education for sustainable development. *Environmental Education Research, 21*(2), 173–182.

Ideland, M. (2016). The action-competent child: Responsibilization through practices and emotions in environmental education. *Knowledge Cultures, 4*(2), 95–112.

Ideland, M. (2017). The end of the world and a promise of happiness: Environmental education within the cultural politics of emotions. In T. Popkewitz, J. Diaz, & C. Kirchgasler (Eds.), *A political sociology of educational knowledge: Studies of exclusions and difference*. London: Taylor & Francis.

Jensen, B. B., & Schnack, K. (2006). The action competence approach in environmental education. *Environmental Education Research, 12*(3–4), 471–486.

Johansson, B. (2004). Consumption and ethics in a children's magazine. In H. Brembeck, B. Johansson, & J. Kampmann (Eds.), *Beyond the competent child: Exploring contemporary childhoods in the Nordic welfare societies* (pp. 229–250). Fredriksberg: Roskilde University Press.

Kenway, J., & Youdell, D. (2011). The emotional geographies of education: Beginning a conversation. *Emotion, Space and Society, 4*(3), 131–136.

Lotz-Sisitka, H., Wals, A. E., Kronlid, D., & McGarry, D. (2015). Transformative, transgressive social learning: Rethinking higher education pedagogy in times of systemic global dysfunction. *Current Opinion in Environmental Sustainability, 16*, 73–80.

Manni, A., Sporre, K., & Ottander, C. (2017). Emotions and values—A case study of meaning-making in ESE. *Environmental Education Research, 23*(4), 451–464.

McClintock, A. (1995). *Imperial leather: Race, gender and sexuality in the colonial contest*. New York, NY: Routledge.

McElhinny, B. (2010). The audacity of affect: Gender, race, and history in linguistic accounts of legitimacy and belonging. *Annual Review of Anthropology, 39*, 309–328.

Miller, P., & Rose, N. (2008). *Governing the present*. Cambridge: Polity Press.

Nadesan, M. H. (2010). *Governing childhood into the 21st century: Biopolitical technologies of childhood management and education*. New York: Palgrave Macmillan.

Naturskyddsföreningen. (2013). *Energifallet*. Retrieved June 5, 2015 from http://www.scribd.com/doc/122751716/Energifallet.

Ojala, M. (2015). Hope in the face of climate change: Associations with environmental engagement and student perceptions of teachers' emotion communication style and future orientation. *The Journal of Environmental Education, 46*(3), 133–148.

Persson, M., Sjöström, B., & Johnsson, P. (2007). *Klimatsmart: Din guide till en miljövänligare vardag*. Stockholm: Alfabeta.

Popkewitz, T. S. (2004). The alchemy of the mathematics curriculum: Inscriptions and fabrications of the child. *American Educational Journal, 41*(4), 3–34.

Popkewitz, T. (2009). Globalization as a system of reason: The historical possibility and the political in pedagogical policy and research. *Yearbook of the National Society for the Study of Education, 108*(2), 247–267.

Popkewitz, T. S. (2012). *Cosmopolitanism and the age of school reform: Science, education, and making society by making the child*. Abingdon and New York: Routledge.

Popkewitz, T. S., & Lindblad, S. (2004). Historicizing the future: Educational reform, systems of reason, and the making of children who are the future citizens. *Journal of Educational Change, 5*(3), 229–247.

Rittel, H. W. J., & Webber, M. M. (1973). Dilemmas in a general theory of planning. *Policy Sciences, 4,* 155–169.

Rose, N., & Miller, P. (2010). Political power beyond the state: Problematics of government. *The British Journal of Sociology, 61,* 271–303.

Skolverket. (2011). *Läroplan för grundskolan, förskoleklassen och fritidshemmet 2011.* Stockholm: Skolverket.

WWF. (2012). *Förskolan: För en hållbar framtid.* Av: Margareta Lakén. Solna: WWF.

4

Locally Grown

Abstract The chapter problematizes how sustainability engagement is embedded in a racial, colonial and nationalistic discourses, positioning different kinds of humans, problems and possibilities in different parts of the world; an enlightened, organized We in the global north and a miserable, corrupt, under-developed Them in the global south. In the Swedish discourse the enlightened, helping, environmental hero is always represented by a white person, while those who are in need of help are represented by a person of color—positioned in Asia or Africa. The chapter discusses how environmental engagement has become culturally attached to whiteness and a Western lifestyle. The work for a common future has, ironically, become an excluding practice dividing the world in Us and Them.

Keywords Sustainability engagement · Racism · Colonialism · Nationalism · Polarizing

It is year 2010. I am at the world's fair in Shanghai to train Chinese teachers in the art of teaching for sustainable development. A colleague and I introduce the workshop by telling of a study we conducted in collaboration with the City of Malmö. In the study we asked ten-year-old children to take a stance on a complex environmental issue. The ten-year-olds had to choose, in groups, different everyday ways to reduce carbon dioxide emissions: for example, walking to school instead of going by car, eating only locally grown fruit, or not flying abroad on vacation more than once a year. At that time we were busy analyzing the children's group discussions and we thought we were on the track of something when it came to letting children tackle complex environmental matters in educational settings. Now we were going to disseminate a pedagogic method! The task for the Chinese teachers was to adapt our project to their own context, to formulate alternatives that could get their pupils involved.

After discussions in groups, the teachers presented their results. A group from Beijing suggested that their pupils could work with alternatives that decreased meat consumption and reduced the power of the air conditioning—suggestions that could also be applied in a Swedish context (but might perhaps mean turning down the heating rather than the cooling). We nodded in recognition and said, as the experts we felt like, that this would probably help the pupils in Beijing to get engaged in environmental issues. Then a group from a rural school in western China, on the border with Mongolia, presented its suggestions. Their first alternative for the pupils to discuss was the possibility of riding to school, on a horse instead of a motorbike. The pupils lived in an extensive geographical area and were weekly commuters to school. Here the teachers could see the potential to save carbon dioxide by changing the mode of transport. The other alternative that would invite pupils to discuss the topic was to heat the school with yak dung instead of coal. Now the Swedish experts did not quite know what to say.

This memory has nagged at me for some years now. Perhaps it is because it illuminates some perspectives on the globally cherished practice of education for sustainable development, perspectives that I had not reflected on at that time. First of all, one must ask why *I*, a Swedish researcher, was expected to be able to teach Chinese teachers about education for sustainable development. I knew nothing about their culture, their school, or their teaching assignment. Secondly, the event shows the absurdity, in my eyes, of considering it normal and reasonable that everyone—in every corner of the earth—should change their lifestyle in the name of sustainable development: rich and poor, regardless of the size of their ecological footprint. One can really wonder how it was possible that I—at that particular moment—could position myself as the enlightened and "good" citizen of the world. This was despite the fact that I had just traveled by airplane, halfway around the globe, to talk about Swedish ten-year-olds who had a guilty conscience about eating imported melons, whereas they, the Chinese teachers, were regarded as in need of my knowledge.

A Green Superpower

The visit to Shanghai may serve as an illustration of the talk of Swedish exceptionalism when it comes to environmental issues, that is to say, environmental engagement as a national identity and a nationalistic project. Of course, this also applies to several other "soft" ideological questions, such as gender equality, human rights, and receiving refugees. The idea of Sweden as a green and humanitarian superpower is deep-rooted in the Swedish self-image. Sweden is good at helping: refugee asylum, humanitarian aid, education in developing countries, sustainability projects, and so on. The ideal image of the Swede is close to the cosmopolitan ideal of a global citizen who tries to improve the world with reason, empathy, tolerance, and engagement. There are no doubt similar self-images in other countries. They function as important components of the national community. But this solidarity with the planet and with other people is paradoxical. Once again, good intentions serve to make distinctions, which is also what Thomas Popkewitz (2012) means when he talks of double gestures of inclusion and exclusion, and how the construction of the Other is done by pointing out those who need help, those who need to be "saved" by the people who are inside the category of normal people (see also Nordvall & Dahlstedt, 2009). Magnus Dahlstedt writes:

> All people in principle are given the chance to make use of all the offers and benefits in society, but only on set conditions. The boundaries around the community are open, negotiable, but at the same time closed. (Dahlstedt, 2010, p. 38)

In the introduction to this book there is a quotation from Wendy Brown (2006, p. 4) that I would like to remind readers of; it was about how good intentions and actions help to orchestrate meaning and dictate the positions and conditions for who we are to be—often with unintentional (?) and problematic consequences. One unintended effect of our journey to Shanghai to train Chinese teachers in ESE is that one simultaneously creates a We (who can) and a They (who need to be taught). This is significant not least for how We view the world, our own position in relation to others.

In this chapter I want to show how sustainable development is used in the making of a national identity and thereby also the Others. The starting point is that categorizations, as well as nationalist and racist representations, do not always arise from evil intentions, but can exist regardless of how good the intention might be. They exist beyond any individual's motives. Perhaps it is even the case that the ideas of Us and Them that are inherent in the taken-for-granted good action are the most "dangerous," in Foucault's sense. They are allowed to ravage freely under a protective shield of good intentions because our mental guard is lowered (Pripp & Öhlander, 2012).[1]

The production of national identity involves a great many different characteristics that together create a kind of imagined national community (Anderson, 2006). My example, Sweden, is described in many contexts as a green superpower with a particular focus on innovations in environmental technology. Swedishness sticks to environmental engagement, engineering and entrepreneurship. But the creation of Swedishness also includes specific values and attributes that we regard as typically Swedish—such as whiteness and rationality. Sometimes my country is described, with some sense of irony, as the most modern country in the world; the center of modernity. This is of course a flattering description, but just as other good intentions this discourse of Swedish environmentalism makes up differences between Us and the Other. Let me give you a similar example of a good intention

---

[1]Elaborated analyses of ESE in relation to racism and nationalism can be found in Ideland and Malmberg (2014), Ideland and Tröhler (2015).

constructing differences. Feminism has recently become a symbol of a distinction between enlightened white people and those who are categorized as more conservative, repressive Others, such as Muslims, because they repress women or do not accept homosexuals. An extreme example is seen when right-wing populist parties—whose ideology is based on differentiating between people—hold Pride parades to show off an identity that is counter to life as a Muslim. A less radical example is an article printed on the debate page of the major Swedish daily *Sydsvenskan*, where two Social Democratic politicians wrote a piece under the heading "Nothing is more un-Swedish than looking down on another person because of his or her religion or skin color" (Ygeman & Schönström, 2015). White Swedes regard themselves as tolerant, and that very categorization constructs categories of Us and Them. As Sara Ahmed (2014) describes it, anti-racism can be viewed as a new form of white pride (see also Hübinette, 2014; Hübinette & Lundström, 2011).

Perhaps not quite as ironic, but close to it, one can also see how sustainable development is constructed as specifically Swedish competence that must be spread to the rest of the world—above all to countries with a small ecological footprint. White—and Swedish—pride derives from the sense that the eco-certified person is "from here," being locally grown.

Exporting Swedish Exceptionalism

As mentioned above, there is a long tradition that what is sometimes called the Western world feels called upon to educate less knowledgeable people in the southern hemisphere, particularly in Africa south of the Sahara and in southeast Asia. Anne McClintock (1995) has described, for example, how education was a strategy in the European colonization of Africa and Asia, and also how a narrative of "enlightening the savages" was allowed to legitimize colonial violence. By emphasizing the narrative of the "development" that took place under the colonial powers more than the narratives about physical, mental, and geographical abuses, the colonial powers stand out in a better light. We saw in the introduction that this, "the single story", told from developmental and educational perspectives hides colonial violences of different kinds—physical as well as epistomological. Coloniality is closely associated with the idea of modern rationality, which also seems to encompass the idea that the West knows what is best for everyone (Hall, 1992). This notion persists in the discourse of education for sustainable development and is expressed through what Noel Gough has addressed as epistemological imperialism:

> The global reach of European imperialism has given Western science the appearance of universal truth and rationality, and many people (regardless of their location) assume that it is a form of knowledge that lacks the cultural fingerprints that seem much more conspicuous in knowledge systems that have retained their ties to specific localities. (Gough, 2002, p. 1223)

This can also be described in Spivak's (1988) words on epistemic violence: how concepts of knowledge, civilization, and education have been used to undermine non-Western methods or approaches to knowledge. The world is conquered by defining what is important—not to say indispensable—knowledge. This is done through the privilege of defining the truth and thus exercising power, to invoke Foucault once again (1980).

When it comes to education for sustainable development, there is a clear epistemological imperialism, produced and sanctioned, for instance, by different UN organs such as UNEP and UNESCO, the organizations that propagate for the call in *Agenda 21* for everyone, everywhere on earth, to strive for sustainable development—regardless of lifestyle and ecological footprint. I should say that I do not think that the United Nations is deliberately guilty of epistemological imperialism; this is an effect of a global harmonization of educational systems (Tröhler, 2009). This harmonization is seen in international measures of knowledge such as PISA tests and in EU projects to develop models for pursuing teaching, but also in the globalization policy concerning ESE. Whether there actually is harmonization, or if it is a transnational imaginary where the global policy is transformed into local practice, is difficult say anything general about. Yet there is a desire; Pasi

Sahlberg (2011) has coined the term GERM as an acronym for Global Education Reform Movement, that is to say, an idea that educational ideals and methods can be spread and translated regardless of culture (Sellar, 2015, pp. 140f.). But the result is that it "infects" the local practices (c.f. McKenzie, 2012).

Besides the UN organs, the World Wide Fund for Nature, WWF, is a powerful actor in the harmonization of environmental and sustainability education. The WWF is one of the oldest and biggest environmental organizations, deeply involved in nature conservation projects all over the world, for instance in saving the organization's mascot, the panda, and other species from extermination.[2] The WWF was founded in 1961. The aim then was to rescue endangered paradises in Asia and Africa from devastation after (allegedly enlightened) European colonial powers had left them. The founders of the organization came from the northwestern part of the world, but the endangered paradises were somewhere else, in nature that belonged to someone else, and this was the nature that was to be saved. There was a powerful belief that enlightenment would prevent this approaching disaster (Ideland & Tröhler, 2015).

This movement took place entirely outside the formal education system and was geared to campaigns for specific projects. It was not until the late 1980s and early 1990s, with the Brundtland Report and *Agenda 21*, that the WWF acquired a more pronounced educational strategy. A report from 1989 pointed out that projects which had focused on a particular endangered species had a "success rate" of roughly 55%, whereas educational projects had been 100% successful (Schwarzenbach, 2011, p. 264). Here I make no claim whatever to be able to explain what was measured or how it could be measured, or what is meant by succeeding 55 or 100%. What is interesting in this context is that it was during this period, as we saw above, that mankind was clearly singled out as the cause of environmental problems, and education and enlightenment

---

[2] I have previously described and analyzed the export of education by the WWF in the book chapter "Calling for Sustainability: WWF's Global Agenda and Educating Swedish Exceptionalism" (Ideland & Tröhler, 2015).

were held up as the solution to the problems. This phenomenon is not restricted to sustainability issues; it is a global policy that education should be an agent of change. During the same period, for instance, the OECD started its international PISA surveys—because school was regarded as crucial for economic success—and one school reform after the other was introduced in Sweden (management by objectives, transfer of responsibility for school from the state to local government, etc.). This was not just to solve the problems of school, but also because education is seen as the way to a desired society. Responsibility for the world is placed on the shoulders of pupils and teachers, as is well illustrated by a quotation from the international website of the WWF:

> To be perfectly honest with you, teachers are quite possibly our #1 customers. It is through you—what you teach, how you teach—that we can quite possibly have the biggest impact on our combined efforts to conserve the majesty of our one and only planet. (WWF, 2014)

What happens in schools is significant for something as big as preserving "the majesty of our one and only planet." This is no little demand to make of school, even though it is done in the form of a "tribute" to teachers. For WWF Sweden this educationalization of the organization involved measures on the home front (to be described below) but also in selected areas in other parts of the world. In a 116-page booklet, *From Vision to Lesson: Education for Sustainable Development in Practice* (Östman, Svanberg, & Aaro-Östman, 2013), WWF Sweden reports and elaborates on ESD projects in countries around Lake Victoria in East Africa, in Mongolia, India, and the Malaysian area of Borneo—the same areas where "endangered paradises" were considered in need of protection when WWF was founded. Education is described (and justified) here as the golden road to sustainable development (SD):

> The importance of education when dealing with SD challenges is obvious. If we take into account that pupils communicate what they have learned in school to their parents and relatives, the estimation is that between 50–70% of a country's population can be reached. (Östman et al., 2013, p. 6)

WWF Sweden is one example of Swedish educational aid in Africa. In this discourse white Swedes are situated as those who teach or even help others to learn, whereas indigenous Africans are those in need of education (Ideland & Tröhler, 2015; Nordvall & Dahlstedt, 2009). The *From Vision to Lesson* report quotes teachers in the various countries, letting them describe the success of the education, how they have developed. For example, it offers a quotation from Indonesia: "Teachers expressed their satisfaction at having developed a new role as teachers: Now we can explain things as knowledgeable resource persons" (Östman et al., 2013, p. 71), and quotes a similar statement from Mongolia: "We have developed the ability to practice this knowledge in our teaching" (p. 71). The Swedish way of addressing sustainability issues comes with a touch of modernity and rationality.

Coloniality and the Modern Project

It is worth noting that all projects described in *From Vision to Lesson* were carried out and reported on by three white Swedish experts, paid for by Sida (the Swedish International Development Cooperation Agency) and organized by WWF Sweden, not by WWF India or Uganda. However, the authors express awareness of the power relations between the educating Swedes and the non-Swedes in need of help to learn. They make a serious attempt to escape epistemological imperialism (cf. Gough, 2002). Nevertheless, this illustrates the core of the difficulties of escaping the colonial gaze in globalized efforts to harmonize education—the ESD practice is stuck in an "Otherness machinery" (Ideland & Malmberg, 2014). Through this machinery, differences between Us and Them are repeatedly (re)constructed within a colonial power structure (McClintock, 1995) in which the represented Other lacks a voice and agency. The irony—that the report is about people with a large ecological footprint trying to get people with a small footprint to improve—is not addressed. On the contrary, those with a small ecological footprint say that they have been "developed" into knowledgeable people with a greater understanding of sustainability. Even though it seems to be done in collaboration, one can clearly discern epistemological violence, as Western knowledge is superior in the hierarchy (cf. McKenzie, 2012). The global perspective, based on the sympathetic attitude that we are all part of the same world, serves as a distinction.

First of all, this is made possible in that, as usual, it is white people who have the preferential right of interpretation in the Western world, and speak about the Other, who becomes the subject of the Western narrative, at best quoted but otherwise without an independent voice. The creation of Us and Them concerns who is permitted to tell the story of education for sustainable development, and who is the story. Spivak (1988), like Donna Haraway (2004), problematizes who represents and who is represented—that the person telling the story becomes the actor while the person about whom the story is told remains an object. The subaltern's voice is not heard (Spivak, 1988). It is silenced through the epistemic violence of not recognizing it as "reasonable," "rational," or "scientific" (cf. Haraway, 2004, p. 88). Or as Santiago Castro-Gómez (2002, p. 269) puts it when discussing coloniality as the other face of modernity:

> Modernity is an alterity-generating machine that, in the name of reason and humanism, excludes from its imaginary the hybridity, multiplicity, ambiguity, and contingency of different forms of life.

How can we understand how this is possible inside ESE, a discourse emphasizing the common—our common home, our common future? We need to think of education in terms of a project of modernity; the rationalization and "disenchantment" of society, as the sociologist Max Weber (2009) conceptualizes it. Important processes in the rationalization of the society were, for instance, an organization of society based on what is seen as rational decisions as opposed to beliefs. Popkewitz (2012) emphasizes how education came to play an important role in the fostering of rational, problem-solving citizens during the rise of modernity. But in that process, specific types of people were being differentiated. A strong connection between industrial (technological) development and colonialism can be illustrated through Weber's work (in Hobson, 2004; see also McClintock, 1995). He positioned modernity in the Occident and its opposite, tradition, in the Orient in what he describes as the "great rationality divide." For instance, the Occident (modernity) is described in terms of rational (public) law, the rational-legal (and democratic) state, rational science and Protestant ethics, and the emergence of the rational individual. On the other hand, the Orientalist (tradition) is described in terms of ad hoc (private) law, the patrimonial (oriental despotic) state, mysticism, repressive religion, and the predominance of collectivity. Western science and Orient unreason were—and are—a narrative making up what is universal knowledge, myths, and which bodies in terms of race and nationality are culturally attached to ideas of being scientific versus unscientific, modern versus traditional. As Said (1978) has taught us, Orient and Occident worked as oppositional terms, so that the Orient was constructed as a negative inversion of Western culture. Taking Weber's perspective on the Occident and the Orient, the West and the Rest, or the Global North and the Global South, it might seem natural that the rational mind was considered as a "gift" brought by the imperial powers to the colonies; a "helping" and civilizing mission (Seth, 2009, p. 373). But the "help" can also be seen as imperial acts imposing differences between people and exercising a kind of epistemic violence (Spivak, 1988)—in the past but also today (Ideland, in press).

Now I shall willingly declare that I know very little about what really happens in the schools in Mongolia, Borneo, and Uganda that were included in the project described above, described in the report *From Vision to Lesson*. Actually I know nothing at all. Perhaps the Swedish ESE model was resisted. It is probably reformulated to something the participants possess; the objects become subjects. Perhaps the subaltern's voice is heard. Anyhow, my interest rather concerns what happens here, in Sweden and in the West, through the images that are communicated about people and living conditions at different places in the world and their need for education. These narratives become elements in the construction of Swedish exceptionalism, a sense of superiority in relation to the Other. It is a concrete example of the paradox of solidarity (Nordvall & Dahlstedt, 2009) and the double gesture of inclusion and exclusion, where the good intention itself serves to exclude and differentiate (Popkewitz, 2012).

The notion of what knowledge is thus interacts with ideas about different geographical places (non-West) but also with ideas about which bodies are associated with the place. Nationality and race interact, as notions about different places in the world are attached to a specific skin color (Puwar, 2004; Villenas & Angeles, 2013). Swedish exceptionalism is therefore also (re)produced through the Swedish racial norm for skin color; whiteness. Nationality and race have stuck together (Ladson-Billings, 1998). And there are a number of attributes sticking to whiteness that have nothing to do with biological constitution but that condition people's possibilities.

Fostering National Exceptionalism at Home

The differentiation takes place not merely through reports from other places or in relation to the Others as subjects. Swedish exceptionalism is also produced through seemingly innocent texts and images describing Swedish educational contexts and their relations to other Nations. One example is the following extract from an inspirational material about Swedish schools collaborating in environmental and sustainability education with the WWF:

Keeping South Africa alive in Falun

Hosjöskolan (Hosjö School) in Falun has for 10 years collaborated with two school classes in South Africa. They keep in touch via sms [text messages], Facebook, and sometimes letters. In connection with Earth Hour in March 2010, the Hosjö class sent letters and drawings in which they described what one can do to not negatively affect the environment. It was exciting for the kids to learn that countries in different continents think similarly and feel the sense of community—we are strong together! A headmaster in South Africa wrote: "I love to work with you in Sweden since everything we do with you turns into gold!" One of the African schools is lacking resources and therefore finds it difficult to answer the letters. It doesn't matter that much, since the pupils at Hosjö school instead then develop the ability to "give." The other school, with almost only white students and teachers, is always contributing with their thoughts and works. It is important for them to know that schools in Sweden are there for them and that the contact remains. (WWF, 2010, p. 74)

I claim that this text simultaneously constructs a world citizen, Swedish (white) exceptionalism, and the Other in need of support. On the one hand, "togetherness" and equity are emphasized, with reference to being strong together and a sense of community. Nevertheless, differences (and power relations) between Sweden and South Africa, white and black, orchestrate the story. Different cultural characteristics stick to different nationalities and races (Ahmed, 2010). Constructions of blacks as non-developed and poor are made by telling the reader about a probably black (skin color is not explicitly stated) South African school that lacks resources. The white school, on the other hand, is described as a little bit more equal to the Swedish school, and they contribute with their work. Race becomes a boundary marker, carrying beliefs about economical possibilities, enlightenment, competence, and technological development.

Furthermore, national differences are constructed through the quotation from the African headmaster about Sweden turning things into gold, as well as the last lines showing the South Africans' need for contact and knowing that "schools in Sweden are there for them." The opposite is not mentioned. Finally, Swedish exceptionalism is emphasized in the mention of how the pupils learn to give and help—a marker for a civilized society with modern, competent citizens (cf. Brown, 2006; Ideland & Tröhler, 2015).

The discourse of Swedish exceptionalism on environmental issues, as has been discussed above as well, operates throughout the ESE material studied, as do other societal practices, such as recycling cans and bottles. In several school textbooks it is stated that "Sweden is world champion of recycling" (SO.S Geografi, 2012, p. 317; Håll Sverige Rent, 2011, p. 11). And the containers in which to put the bottles and cans are colored like the Swedish national flag in blue and yellow. There you can also simply push a button and perform a good deed—donate the deposit to a charity organization. Repeatedly pointing out how good "Sweden" is at recycling bottles and cans is another element in the construction of Swedish exceptionalism and an imagined community. Returning bottles and cans for the deposit (which also presupposes that you have actually bought the drinks in bottles or cans) is equated with a good action and a part of the national identity construction.

Here one can really talk of how small everyday acts are linked to global issues, as discussed in the chapter "Free-range children." I can understand the point of returning bottles and donating the deposit at the machine. Every little action helps… But why the blue-and-yellow aesthetic? Why the nationalistic touch? This must be understood in relation to the notion of Sweden as the green superpower, as heard time and again in the sustainability discourse: in commercially published textbooks, in advertising, in news articles about Swedish environmental technology, in political debates, and so on. This is despite the fact that Sweden's ecological footprint, as we have seen, is one of the biggest in the world. This rhetoric, in combination with projects aimed at educating for sustainability in the Global South, is a materialization of the power technology of coloniality reproducing patterns of difference and teaching children and youngsters to look at the world with a colonial gaze.

The Western Order

The focus on recycling illustrates how ideas about chaos and order organize the narrative of sustainability (Ideland & Malmberg, 2014). In the creation of a "We," the notion of order is important. We create order in our waste by recycling it, putting it in special containers where it takes on a new value. The garbage is transformed through different sorting processes, from dirt into a valuable object. In the children's world, for example, in the game *Små kloka barn jagar miljöbovar* ("Clever Children Chase Environmental Polluters"), one can earn money by collecting and sorting waste. The aim of the game is to be able to turn a dirty game board into a clean one and say: "Just think if all the environmental villains behaved like me, imagine how nice the city would be!" A similar game, *Sopberget* ("The Waste Mountain") can also be won by placing garbage in the right bin. Without any evidence, I would claim that by far the most common environmental projects in Swedish schools and preschools have to do with waste. Batteries are collected, food waste in preschools is placed in the compost, preschool teachers attach different materials to a plank that is buried in the ground to illustrate what decomposes and what does not.

Domestic waste for recycling is brought to school or preschool to be transformed into creative projects. And so on. But even in the adult world the eco-certified person can help to transform dirt into something valuable. Plastic, aluminum, food waste, paper, and even sewage can be transformed into valuable products such as new packages, but also into something completely different such as biogas or polar fleece sweaters. The flea market is another example of a place where someone's trash can be someone else's treasure. The eco-certified person organizes the waste, transforms it from dirt into something—educationally, aesthetically, or economically—valuable.

The anthropologist Mary Douglas (1966/2002) showed in the 1960 how dirt, nausea, and taboo can be understood in terms of "matter out of place." Hair is considered as beautiful on the head, but not on a woman's legs, and if it gets into food it is even transformed into something disgusting. Blood should stay inside the body, unless it is transplanted in a controlled manner. With the help of ordered rituals, something that is understood as dirt can be transformed into something clean, as with the recycling of waste. For instance, food waste is composted to become nutritious soil or cardboard packaging can become a statue at preschool. Dirt is purified, and this cultural division between dirt and purity is an important tool for organizing our understanding of the world and of people in the ESE discourse. There is a frequently recurring narrative in the textbooks about how the Others live in the dirt. In the teaching material words like "dirt" and "pollution" stick to bodies of color in Asia and Africa. Virtually all texts with a global perspective on global issues, as desired by the curriculum, are illustrated with black people in (chaotic, non-ordered) dirty environments. Sometimes the pictures are printed without comment, at other times with captions about the problems with dirt in Africa and Asia, often pointing out the lack of clean water. One example is a photo of a boy wading up to his waist in incredibly filthy water, accompanied by the text:

> It is common that children around the world die from diarrhea. The reason is often that they have no access to anything but contaminated water. Here is a boy looking for food among garbage in dirty water in Djakarta, the capital of Indonesia. (*SO.S Samhälle*, 2012, p. 350)

The descriptions and pictures will probably be recognizable. The Other who lives in dirt and chaos is, as mentioned above, a recurrent narrative—not just in relation to sustainable development and the environment. One must question how this message affects the way children and adults view the world and people in different national and geographical places and of different races. In the name of the good intention to help people living in messy and dirty environments, texts and pictures communicate the sticky feeling of disgust by repeating the narrative. The point is that the disgust should be transformed into pity for the Other—the person who lives in dirt. Pitying thus becomes a part of the (re)production of sorting and racifying bodies (Ahmed, 2004; Matias & Zembylas, 2014). We are not used to see Western, white people up to their waists in filth. On the contrary, they are culturally constructed as world champions at returning deposit packaging and cheerfully sorting their waste. Karen Bradley (2009) has also shown in her dissertation how immigrants to Sweden often are singled out as those who need to learn how to recycle. Orderly waste management becomes part of the acquisition of a civilized identity.

The message: We in the West know how to organize. Not just trash. We also have laws and ordinances, curricula and other means to help in the work for sustainable development (*Hållbar utveckling: Hotet mot vår miljö*, 2005, p. 35). The Others have no system (of the Swedish kind) and are therefore viewed as a problem. One example comes from a civics textbook for the upper level (grades 7–9) where two descriptions of female political leaders illustrate how a distinction is made between Us and Them by separating chaos from order (cf. Ideland & Malmberg, 2014). The first example is about the then president of Liberia, Ellen Sirleaf Johnson. The intention to focus on African development and a female president was most likely well-meaning, but the text is still othering:

Liberia's president, Ellen Sirleaf Johnson, tries to lift her country out of corruption and heal wounds after many years of war through placing well-educated women in prominent political positions. Liberia is one of the world's poorest countries and after 14 years of civil war, almost all of

the men in leadership positions are corrupt, which is why Ellen Sirleaf
Johnson turned to these women. She received the Nobel Prize for Peace
in 2011 for her actions. (*SO.S Samhälle*, 2012, p. 342)

The description and picture of Sirleaf Johnson can be considered as a
leak in a hegemonic societal and educational discourse, since she is a
black, female, African politician who is mainly in the company of
white, Western politicians in the empirical material. The representa-
tion of her is organized within a strongly gendered discourse, portray-
ing women as healing wounds and being reliable in contrast to corrupt
men. Besides this, she is also represented as non-white, non-Western by
words such as "tries to," "corrupt," and "poorest countries." A description of a white, female, European politician in the same book serves as a
contrasting example:

Gro Harlem Brundtland, prime minister of Norway during the 1980's
and 1990's, is an important person for the idea of sustainable development. She led the work in the group that presented the report "Our
Common Future" at the UN conference about environment and development in Rio de Janeiro in 1992. (*SO.S Samhälle*, 2012, p. 346)

Brundtland doesn't "try to," she has "led the work" and is described as
an "important person." Neither is Brundtland's work described in terms
of any problems, even though it is easy to imagine that there must have
been differences of opinion when the influential report was written. The
description of Sirleaf Johnson is another example of the double gestures of inclusion and exclusion. The good intention to let students read
about a successful Liberian politician is stuck in the Otherness machinery. The intention to explain difficulties in Liberia becomes a part of the
discourse that demarcates the West from the Rest and reproduces the
image of Europe as more effective, with higher morals and more democratic than the rest of the world. Mannion, Biesta, Priestley, and Ross
(2011, p. 452) write about a taken-for-granted view that it is We who,
after all, supposedly lead in the process of globalization—to ensure the
order of the world.

Eco-Certified Bodies

Let me return once again to my own life as a researcher, and the structures that I reproduce through my actions. The chapter began with a story from Shanghai which illustrated how I have become more "enlightened" about colonial practices in and through ESE. A closing story may illustrate how the problem remains, despite my enlightenment through studies of postcolonial theory. In the fall of 2014 I was invited to be the keynote speaker at a conference on Science and Technology Education, to lecture about the topic of this chapter—how the discourse of education for sustainable development (re)produces differences between Us and Them. The title was *Global Responsibility or Eco-certified Nationalism? About Impossibilities of Non-colonial ESD*. As the now enlightened expert that I felt I was at the lectern, I described my change and my new insights to a truly international audience at a conference hotel in Kuching, Malaysia. Afterward one of the listeners was indignant, a black woman from South Africa who had tried for many years to put across a similar message. How come I—a white, European, Swedish woman had been appointed as the keynote speaker, the invited "expert" of racism and colonialism. Although I myself have *never* been a victim of racism in my privileged position. Why was I given the position of expert on colonial structures and racism? Why did I accept it? Was it—as Ahmed (2007, 2012) points out—because antiracism functions as an important part of the identity construction of an enlightened person? Why do I continue to take this position here, in a confession where I can ease my conscience?

Alan Pred writes in the book *Even in Sweden* that even here, in a country that is stereotypically described as a paradise for social justice, a model country for solidarity and "civilized behavior toward others," racism is flourishing (Pred, 2000, p. 6). Bodies and people are racified, that is to say, marked as non-white which means that societal and political possibilities are conditional—depending on who you are, how your body appears, which language you speak etc. Instead of recognizing that distinctions are made, the "color-blind" (Bonilla-Silva, 2003) idea of a non-racist country survives. Yet we can see how even good intentions such as ESE (re)produce a nationalist and racist way of seeing and understanding the world; coloniality works as a power technology in ESE. This takes place, not least of all, through epistemological violence, as certain knowledge machinery is rewarded above others—regardless of the environmental impact it represents. Through the talk of knowledge and order, a claim is made to know the truth about the good life and the good citizen, and about those who endanger the future with their way of life. It also takes place in the way that white bodies are *always* allowed to represent the environmental heroes in the textbooks, while non-white bodies are represented only with reference to environmental problems, dirt, and disgust. The eco-certified body is obviously white in the Swedish ESE discourse.

The strong trust in Sweden, together with representations of white people as educated, technologically developed, and orderly, and with black bodies wallowing in dirt, probably does not have any colonial or racist *intentions*, but it does have *effects*. By constantly reading about these differences, children are trained in their colonial gaze on the world. The good intentions of talking about sustainability problems in different parts of the world, and of teaching sustainability to people "somewhere else," ultimately reproduce colonial, nationalist, and racist structures in society.

References

Ahmed, S. (2004). Affective economies. *Social Text, 22*(2), 117–139.
Ahmed, S. (2007). The language of diversity. *Ethnic and Racial Studies, 30*(2), 235–256.
Ahmed, S. (2010). *The promise of happiness*. Durham: Duke University Press.
Ahmed, S. (2012). *On being included: Racism and diversity in institutional life.* Durham and London: Duke University Press.
Ahmed, S. (2014). *The cultural politics of emotion* (2nd ed.). Edinburgh: Edinburgh University Press.
Anderson, B. (2006). *Imagined communities: Reflections on the origin and spread of nationalism*. Brooklyn: Verso Books.

Bonilla-Silva, E. (2003). 'New racism,' color-blind racism, and the future of Whiteness in America. In A.W. Doane & E. Bonilla-Silva, (Eds.), *White out: The continuing significance of racism* (pp. 271–284). New York and London: Routledge.

Bowden, R. (2005). *Hållbar utveckling: Hotet mot miljön.* Stockholm: Liber.

Bradley, K. (2009). *Just environments: Politicising sustainable urban development.* Stockholm: KTH.

Brown, W. (2006). *Regulating aversion: Tolerance in the age of identity and empire.* Princeton, NJ: Princeton University Press.

Castro-Gómez, S. (2002). The social sciences, epistemic violence, and the problem of the "invention of the other". *Nepantla: Views from South, 3*(2), 269–285.

Dahlstedt, M. (2010). Hårda nypor för ett mjukt samhälle? Om medialisering och rasifiering i utspelspolitikens Sverige. *Sociologisk Forskning, 47*(3), 35–56.

Douglas, M. (1966/2002). *Purity and danger: An analysis of concepts of pollution and taboo.* London: Taylor & Francis.

Foucault, M. (1980). *Power/knowledge: Selected interviews and other writings 1972–1977* (C. Gordon, Ed.). Harlow: Harvester Press.

Gough, N. (2002). Thinking/acting locally/globally: Western science and environmental education in a global knowledge economy. *International Journal of Science Education, 24*(11), 1217–1237.

Hall, S. (1992). The west and the rest: Discourse and power. In S. Hall & B. Geiben (Eds.), *Formations of modernity* (pp. 15–30). Cambridge, UK: Polity Press.

Håll Sverige Rent. (2011). *Blixtpatrullens äventyr.* Author: L. Adelsköld.

Haraway, D. J. (2004). *The Haraway reader.* New York: Routledge.

Hobson, J. M. (2004). *The Eastern origins of Western civilisation.* Cambridge: Cambridge University Press.

Hübinette, T. (2014). Racial stereotypes and Swedish antiracism: A Swedish crisis of multiculturalism? In L. Jensen & K. Loftsdóttir (Eds.), *Crisis in the Nordic nations and beyond: At the intersection of environment, finance and multiculturalism* (pp. 69–85). Farnham: Ashgate.

Hübinette, T., & Lundström, C. (2011). Sweden after the recent election: The double-binding power of Swedish whiteness through the mourning of the loss of 'old Sweden' and the passing of 'good Sweden'. *NORA—Nordic Journal of Feminist and Gender Research, 19*(1), 42–52.

Ideland, M. (in press). Science, Coloniality, and "the Great Rationality Divide". How Practices, Places, and Persons Are Culturally Attached to

One Another in Science Education. Science and Education. https://doi.org/10.1007/s11191-018-0006-8.

Ideland, M., & Malmberg, C. (2014). Our common world belongs to 'Us': Constructions of otherness in education for sustainable development. *Critical Studies in Education, 55*(3), 369–386.

Ideland, M., & Tröhler, D. (2015). Calling for sustainability: WWF's global agenda and educating Swedish exceptionalism. In D. Tröhler & T. Lenz (Eds.), *Trajectories in the development of modern school systems: Between the national and the global* (pp. 199–212). Abingdon and New York: Routledge.

Ladson-Billings, G. (1998). Just what is critical race theory and what's it doing in a nice field like education? *International Journal of Qualitative Studies in Education, 11*(1), 7–24.

Mannion, G., Biesta, G., Priestley, M., & Ross, H. (2011). The global dimension in education and education for global citizenship: Genealogy and critique. *Globalisation, Societies and Education, 9*(3–4), 443–456.

Matias, C. E., & Zembylas, M. (2014). 'When saying you care is not really caring': Emotions of disgust, whiteness ideology, and teacher education. *Critical Studies in Education, 55*(3), 319–337.

McClintock, A. (1995). *Imperial leather: Race, gender and sexuality in the colonial contest.* New York, NY: Routledge.

McKenzie, M. (2012). Education for y'all: Global neoliberalism and the case for a politics of scale in sustainability education policy. *Policy Futures in Education, 10*(2), 165–177.

Nordvall, H., & Dahlstedt, M. (2009). Folkbildning i (av)koloniseringens skugga: Demokrati, nationella mytologier och solidaritetens paradoxer. *Utbildning och Demokrati, 18*(3), 29–47.

Östman, L., Svanberg, S., & Aaro-Östman, E. (2013). *From vision to lesson: Education for sustainable development in practice.* Stockholm, Sweden: WWF.

Popkewitz, T. S. (2012). *Cosmopolitanism and the age of school reform: Science, education, and making society by making the child.* Abingdon and New York: Routledge.

Pred, A. (2000). *Even in Sweden: Racisms, racialized spaces, and the popular geographical imagination.* Berkeley: University of California Press.

Pripp, O., & Öhlander, M. (2012). Att uppfatta rasism i Sverige. Om glassreklam och normstrider. In T. Hübinette, H. Hörnfeldt, F. Farahani, & R. L. Rosales (Eds.), *Om ras och vithet i det samtida Sverige.* Tumba: Mångkulturellt centrum.

Puwar, N. (2004). *Space invaders, race, gender and bodies out of place*. New York: Berg.

Sahlberg, P. (2011). The fourth way of Finland. *Journal of Educational Change, 12*(2), 173–185.

Said, E. (1978). *Orientalism: Western representations of the Orient*. New York: Pantheon.

Schwarzenbach, A. (2011). *Saving the world's wildlife: WWF—The first 50 years*. London, UK: Profile.

Sellar, S. (2015). A feel for numbers: Affect, data and education policy. *Critical Studies in Education, 56*(1), 131–146.

Seth, S. (2009). Putting knowledge in its place: Science, colonialism, and the postcolonial. *Postcolonial Studies, 12*(4), 373–388.

SO.S Geografi. (2012). Stockholm: Liber. Authors: L. Lindberg & S. Mårtensson.

SO.S Samhälle. (2012). Stockholm: Liber. Authors: U. Andersson, P. Ewert, & U. Hedengren.

Spivak, G. C. (1988). Can the subaltern speak? In C. Nelson & L. Grossberg (Eds.), *Marxism and the interpretation of culture* (pp. 271–313). Basingstoke, UK: Macmillan Education.

Tröhler, D. (2009). Harmonizing the educational globe: World polity, cultural features, and the challenges to educational research. *Studies in Philosophy and Education, 29*(1), 7–29.

Villenas, S. A., & Angeles, S. L. (2013). Race talk and school equity in local print media: The discursive flexibility of whiteness and the promise of race-conscious talk. *Discourse: Studies in the Cultural Politics of Education, 34*(4), 510–530.

Weber, M. (2009). *From Max Weber: Essays in sociology*. Abingdon: Routledge.

WWF. (2010). *Skola på hållbar väg – skolors arbete inom hållbar utveckling*. Solna: WWF.

WWF. (2014). *A collection of articles, ideas and links for lesson planning?* Retrieved May 5, 2014, from http://wwf.panda.org/about_our_earth/teacher_resources/.

Ygeman, A., & Schönström, A. (2015). Ingenting är mer osvenskt än att se ner på en annan människa på grund av dennes religion eller hudfärg. *Sydsvenskan, 3*(6), 2015.

5

Natural—With No Artificial Additives

Abstract The chapter analyzes what it means that the eco-certified child is repeatedly described as a nature-loving person—one who likes being outdoors, discovering and caring for the nature. But to pass as environmentally friendly nature-lover, not any way of being in the nature counts. On the contrary, nature is here understood as a metaphorical place organizing desirable and undesirable ways of living organized by cultural norms for race and social class; all inside the discourse of Western modernity. With help from Nirmal Puwar it is discussed how different places—the sacral nature respectively the urban ghetto—are culturally attached to different kinds of people, and how the ones crossing the borders become "space invaders" who are disturbing the sense of an imagined community.

Keywords Cultural norms · Western hegemony · Migration

I have a dog, a lagotto romagnolo. The Swedish life with a dog is often associated with walks in the forest and a feeling for animals and nature. The eco-certified person can have a dog, as it is a good fit for the cultural thesis of what an "environmentally friendly" person is supposed to

© The Author(s) 2019

M. Ideland, *The Eco-Certified Child*, Palgrave Studies in Education
and the Environment, https://doi.org/10.1007/978-3-030-00199-5_5

be like. But is it really so environmentally friendly? A few years ago a report on a New Zealand study was published. The researchers had calculated the carbon dioxide emissions caused by dog owning and compared it with other everyday actions, such as driving a car. The scientists Robert Vale and Brenda Vale used a measure similar to the carbon footprint. Based on calculations of the production process for dog food and how much an average dog eats, they arrived at a footprint of 0.84 hectares per year. This can be compared with how much energy a Toyota Land Cruiser consumes if it is driven 10,000 km a year. This footprint turned out to be roughly half that of the dog, 0.41 hectares. Not even a cat appears to be particularly environmentally friendly to feed—cat food causes as much carbon dioxide emissions as a VW Golf according to Vale and Vale. This means that a SUV—in a Swedish context a symbol of environmental degradation—according to this calculation is less of a climate threat than a dog (or perhaps even a cat) (Adlercreutz, 2012).

The comparison between owning a SUV and owning a dog highlights the question of symbols in the discourse of sustainable development and the criteria for the eco-certified child. Although science and technological development structure the discourse, the image of the environmental activist is that of a person who enjoys forest walks and bird-watching more than, say, working in a lab with genetic modification of a crop plant to make it better able to withstand extreme weather. Environmental work has long been synonymous with conserving nature. It has been a question of protecting endangered species, keep the natural clean from litter, and so on. But there is also a strong belief, not least in teaching about the environment and sustainability, that experiences of nature as such lead children and adults to develop a concern for nature and pro-environmental behavior (e.g. Braun & Dierkes, 2017; Ting, Ting, Cheng, & Cheng, 2017). The actual place "out in nature" (in the singular, see Fletcher, 2017 for its complexity) sticks culturally to the environmentally friendly person, and in this chapter, I will discuss both how this discourse has emerged and how it includes and excludes different categories of people.

To be noted; it is a special kind of nature we are talking about. It is the "original" nature that is the symbol of environmental engagement;

in a Swedish context, it is the open landscape, the verdant summer meadow, and the blue sea. Nature's symbolic value, it goes without saying, is exploited by the advertising industry, for example by the certification organization KRAV in its advertisements for choosing organically produced food. During the winter of 2014–2015 they sold macaroni with the aid of the following slogan: "Boil macaroni with birdsong, open landscapes, biological diversity, and unsprayed fields." Parallels can be drawn with Ben & Jerry's trademark, where one can feel good by eating good ice cream. Here the taste of macaroni is supposed to evoke an experience of nature, with birdsong and open landscape. Of course the text should be interpreted as saying that ecological farming preserves these things, but it is also a matter of evoking a sense of nature.

The Natural Child

In preschool and school, nature has a very special meaning. There is a powerful discourse telling that children are closer to nature than adults are—they are simply more natural because they have not yet been "spoiled" by the influence of society and civilization. And the younger they are, the closer they are to the untouched nature. Friedrich Fröbel (1782–1852), who is often held up as the man who founded kindergarten, nourished a strong belief in the primordial and natural child, a plant that could be cultivated with care. He was inspired by the Enlightenment philosopher Rousseau's ideas of the good and free child living close to nature—which at the time was the same as living close to God.[1] Gunilla Halldén (2009), a Swedish researcher in child studies, cites Fröbel and others to demonstrate how nature has become a symbol of the good childhood. Playing in the forest, swimming in the sea, fresh air, all this is part of the idea of the child and childhood. In this discourse, children should not sit inside by their computers, they should go out and play!

---

[1]This has been discussed in a number of dissertations in preschool research. See e.g. Ärlemalm-Hagsér (2013), Sjöstrand-Öhrfelt (2014), Thulin (2011).

The smaller the child is, the more natural and closer to nature it is considered to be. Magdalena Sjöstrand-Öhrfelt, in her dissertation *Barn i natur och natur i barn* ("Children in Nature and Nature in Children," 2015), has described and critically analyzed how outdoor preschool and outdoor pedagogy have emerged as ideals in the Swedish context, how they are culturally legitimized by being held up as the answer to many problems in modernity, such as sedentariness, ill health, unequal gender roles, and so forth. In recent years, also unsustainable development and environmental problems have been cited as arguments for why outdoor activity is meaningful:

> The health discourse, which prescribes that spending time in nature and outdoors benefits children's health, and which has traditionally been strong and prominent in outdoor pedagogy, has now increasingly given way to a discourse about the health of the earth and of nature, and this has now to some extent replaced it as an argument for outdoor pedagogy. (Sjöstrand-Öhrfelt, 2014, p. 114)

The eco-certified child, in other words, has a relationship to natural nature. Merely by being in this place, it is envisaged that children develop ecological literacy, that is, the competence to understand ecosystems and the principles for sustainability, and the ability to "read" nature (Magntorn, 2007; Orr, 1992). Pro-environmental behavior is believed to be fostered because being in nature means looking after it, ultimately giving the energy and resolve to conserve nature (Fletcher, 2015; Mayer, Frantz, Bruehlman-Senecal, & Dolliver, 2009). Those who cannot or do not want to spend time in nature then become "the dangerous children," those who threaten sustainable development. In this discourse the dangerous, undesirable child is described in terms such as ecophobia, ecological alienation (Sjöstrand-Öhrfelt, 2014, p. 40), or even as suffering from "nature deficit disorder," as the American Richard Louv (2005) puts it.[2] In Louv's conceptual apparatus, living at

---

[2]Louv described this first in the book *Last Child in the Woods* (2005). Two years later the same man made the appeal "Leave no child inside" to the US Congress, by analogy with George W. Bush's school reform "No child left behind" (Louv, 2007). For further discussion of this see Sjöstrand-Öhrfelt (2014).

a distance from nature is a diagnosis—which may be said to be an unu-sually strong expression, even though the discourse otherwise clearly (re) produces the desirable child as being close to nature and the dangerous child as being cut off from it.

Nature here becomes at once a place and a metaphor that structures and organizes desirable and undesirable subjectivities, that is to say, ways of being and living (Haraway, 2004, p. 65). The modern society stakes out a place for every individual, and constructs an individual for every place. The place and its inhabitants are closely interwoven. This means that some belong while others become what Nirmal Puwar calls "space invaders":

> However, social spaces are not blank and open for any body to occupy. There is a connection between bodies and space, which is built, repeated and contested over time. While all can, in theory, enter, it is certain types of bodies that are tacitly designated as being the "natural" occupants of specific positions. Some bodies are deemed as having the right to belong, while others are marked out as trespassers, who are, in accordance with how spaces and bodies are imagined (politically, historically and con-ceptually) circumscribed as being "out of place". Not being the somatic norm, they are space invaders. (Puwar, 2004, p. 8)

Puwar cites a number of example of which bodies fit which environ-ments and who becomes what Sara Ahmed (2007) calls invisible and hyper-visible at the same time in a specific context. What falls beyond the somatic norm can be ignored, but it also becomes visible, exposing what is both inside and outside the borders for the notion of desirable citizens.

Go Out!

How are nature and the eco-certified child interwoven in the teach-ing material used in school? Let me take an example from the educa-tional material aimed by Keep Sweden Clean at preschool and the lower level of compulsory school: *Blixtpatrullens äventyr* ("Adventures of the

Lightning Patrol," Håll Sverige Rent, 2011). Accompanied by a picture of children wearing superhero cloaks on a forest excursion, the following text can be read:

> Kalle likes peace and quiet. What he likes best of all is to lie on his back in the grass, looking up at the sky as the clouds float by and the gulls fly.
>
> Benjamin prefers to dance and sing aloud to himself when he is outside. Sometimes he sings to the trees too, because he believes that they like it.
>
> Zoe is often out in the forest. She knows a lot about animals because she has a dog of her own that she has learned to look after.
>
> Kristoffer loves climbing trees and he is really good at that. He can climb big trees, small trees, thick trees, and quite narrow trees too. He knows exactly which branches he can stand on so that he will not damage the tree or fall off. [...]
>
> Josefin likes small creepy things and she brings jars and a magnifying glass so that she can look at all the small animals she finds under stones and in tree stumps.
>
> Siri thinks it's fun to build things. When she is out she makes little houses and boats and dinosaurs out of things she finds in nature. (Håll Sverige Rent 2011, p. 7)

The descriptions of the children in the Lightning Patrol can be read as models of what one "ought to be," cultural theses for the good life in nature (Popkewitz, 2009). The instructions accompanying the material say that these descriptions of fictional characters can serve as a basis for real children to say what they like doing outdoors—what nature does to them. Here we have children with different interests to identify with, presumably in order to avoid stereotypes. The author has also avoided traditional gender roles, for example letting Benjamin dance and Siri build. Yet it is a very homogeneous child that emerges from the overall picture, and one that also agrees with other pictures and descriptions of children who fight for sustainability by going out into nature.

The model for the eco-certified child here is, first of all, the curious, exploring child, always ready with a magnifying glass and a butterfly net, a child that learns about nature and approaches it in search of knowledge. In the Lightning Patrol, we find Josefin and Zoe who view life in a way that, even by preschool standards, is scientific. They learn by being out in nature. Close to this category is Siri, who likes building when she is outdoors; she is the engineer who solves problems and makes things. In Swedish schools, there is a strong link between science, technological development, and sustainable development. The science subjects in school, ever since the general curriculum was introduced in 1962, have had a focus on the conservation of nature with the aid of a scientific attitude and scientific methods of investigation (Hillbur, Ideland, & Malmberg, 2016). This has been formulated in slightly different ways, however. In 1962 it was clearly a matter of nature conservation:

> When teaching in all grades and especially during field trips, teachers should avail themselves of the opportunities that may arise to make pupils realize the importance of conservation and animal welfare. Harm to animals and plants, such as behaving inconsiderately when picking flowers and collecting plants, damaging trees and shrubs in the wild and in plantations, robbing birds' nests, and animal cruelty in all forms, should be held up as something unworthy. […] Schools should stimulate pupils to put up bird houses, and they should have the opportunity to produce them in woodwork classes. (The Royal National Board of Education, 1962, pp. 275f.)

The eco-certified child in 1962 was one who understood and looked after nature, while the Other—a person who was cruel to animals and picked flowers without consideration—was portrayed as "unworthy." The wording seems old-fashioned today, but these are discourses that still organize the ESE practices. Then—as now—science is the main domicile for teaching about the environment and sustainability, and nature is the object of study and protection. Somewhat paradoxically, great hopes are pinned on technological development. In a study that my colleagues and I have conducted with ten-year-olds talking about how they can reduce their carbon dioxide emissions, one can see how the children perceive science and technology as powerful—and unproblematic—instruments for sustainable development. The children speculate about the possibility of airplanes powered by solar cells and technology that can exploit the methane gas from cows' farts (Byrne, Ideland, Malmberg, & Grace, 2014). In the ESE discourse, science and technology are seen as solutions rather than problems (as GMOs, for example, are sometimes described). The link between the scientific revolution, industrialism, colonialism, and pollution that so many have pointed out (see e.g. Harding, 2011; Klein, 2014; McClintock, 1995) is completely invisible in the school teaching material. As we have seen, the negative sides are concealed by a development paradigm in which all progress is good progress, which is also yet another incentive to foster the Other—in order to develop the part of the world which, according to a colonial way of thinking, is underdeveloped.

On the other hand, there are also more "childish" children in the Lightning Patrol, those who run, jump, climb, and swim and are active in a way that "children" are imagined to be in the forest. This too is a clearly desirable subject in the sustainability discourse—it is important to "do things," to be active. In this category we can place, for example, Benjamin, who dances outdoors. Then we have Kalle who just likes hanging out in nature, enjoying and feeling good and experiencing things with all his senses. The children who are out for play and enjoyment fit a romantic notion of nature and children, a strong counter to the child sitting inside at the computer or the tablet. The ideal child of the Lightning Patrol is associated, to a greater or lesser degree, with opposition to excess consumption and computerization—things and behaviors that can be described as artificial additives in the nature discourse. Given the optimism about technology that is so characteristic of the discourse, modern technology in the form of mobile phones, tablets, and computers is paradoxically absent from the teaching material. Traditional technical aids, such as binoculars, magnifying glasses, and butterfly nets, on the other hand, have a "natural" place in nature. They are instruments for activities in the nature. Orvar Löfgren writes:

> In today's society the popularity of a walk in the forest is due not least to this multisensory corporeality. Being in the forest means a feeling of doing something more than just looking at something. To have "been out

in the forest" with the kids rather than visiting the huge toy store on the other side of the freeway is a moral victory. Here comes an active family that does real things. (Löfgren, 1997, p. 55)

Once again: Go out and play! Beware of Nature Deficit Disorder! But, as we saw above in the categorizing of the members of the Lightning Patrol, the eco-certified child is not just a playing child but, perhaps primarily, a learning child. The point of this teaching material is that children will *learn* things, and it is also through this focus that the experience of nature is linked to the responsible, sustainable life. The subtitle of this material about the Lightning Patrol's adventures means "Play and Learn about Littering, Freedom to Roam, and Rubbish as a Resource." Precisely this play/learn combination is central for desirable children according to the cultural thesis of the eco-certified child. Although "just being" in nature is often held up as an action for sustainability, because it gives a "feel for nature," the eco-certified child is additionally always exploring and learning. Sjöstrand-Öhrfelt (2014) describes how two historical threads in the view of children and nature organize the discourse about children's time spent outside at preschool. On the one hand, there is an Anglo-Saxon tradition with the idea that being outdoors strengthens children's character and teaches them that nature is something that can—and should—be conquered and tamed. The scouting movement is an obvious product of this tradition. On the other hand, there is a Nordic tradition based on a romantic notion of nature as a place of recreation, and as an important foundation stone in the national identity. These different discourses meet in the teaching material, shaping the image of a desirable child who, by acquiring a knowledge of nature can both enjoy it and take better care of it.

Nature as a Place for Work

The romantic image of nature goes back to the end of the nineteenth century, when the bourgeoisie colonized the forest. From having been a workplace for farmers and lumberjacks, Swedish nature also became an idyllic recreation place for the bourgeoisie and later the emerging middle class (Frykman & Löfgren, 1987). The idea of nature conservation arose, since nature as a place needed protection from humans with the help of humans. During this period, in 1909 to be exact, the Swedish Society for Nature Conservation (Sveriges Naturskyddsförening) was founded, as a response to this need to conserve and protect nature.[3] This romantic idea of nature can be described as a modern Western, even urban, perspective on nature. It was an attitude that was chiefly (re)produced by people who no longer lived close to nature and were not directly dependent on it, as farmers, hunters, and fishermen were. Nature had become a place for leisure.

Since the start of the twenty-first century, however, there has also been an educational colonization of nature, with nature trails and outdoor pedagogy. It could be said that nature has once again become a workplace, but today it is for children with magnifying glasses, butterfly nets, insect books, and camping stoves. Nature thus positions the child as working, and this sets its stamp on the games they play. It is not just any games that count in the sustainability project; they must be educational and offer opportunities for learning—as in the example "Kim's Rubbishy Game", described in a teaching material for young children:

> If you have a big heap of rubbish that you have collected outside, before you recycle it or dispose of it, you can play this memory game. The teacher prepares the game by putting an amount of rubbish in a square on the ground. The square may be marked with sticks. The children can work in pairs or bigger groups. First let everyone look at the prepared square for a while, and then put something over the square to cover it. Then everyone has to make a square with similar contents. If you want to make it a little more difficult you can also require the right thing to be in the right place in the square. Ensure that there is enough rubbish so that everyone can create identical squares. (Håll Sverige Rent 2011, pp. 9f.)

---

[3]This can be compared with the fact that the WWF was founded as a reaction to the way the European colonial powers in Africa and Asia left the natural paradises to their fate, as discussed in the previous chapter. The WWF did not trust that these places would be properly cared for when the knowledgeable and rational Westerners were no longer there (Ideland & Tröhler, 2015).

Collecting waste becomes a learning, working assignment. A good game also has a good learning goal, likewise becoming another way for education to colonize the experience of nature. This pedagogy also includes learning how to be careful. Kristoffer of the Lightning Patrol, for example, knows "exactly which branches he can stand on so that he will not damage the tree" (Håll Sverige Rent 2011, p. 7). Broken branches here serve as a governing technology, appealing to children to look after nature, and nature becomes a part of the flock for which the individual must take responsibility. In terms of the effect on the environment, on the other hand, it can be unfavorably compared with all the environmental impact that occurs through the consumption by Kristoffer and other eco-certified children when they are not in nature. Let's make a thinking experiment: If Kristoffer wants to give his mother a lovely present, say a silver necklace, what is the environmental impact of the mining for the metal? But the nonaction of not buying a present is also nonperformative—the mining takes place where the child does not see it (of no importance for the child's upbringing) and nonaction entails no work, no active deeds, for the child. Moreover, a present has a good purpose, unlike the act of deliberately breaking off a branch. To use the words of Sara Ahmed (2014), since it feels good to give away a present, it must also—according to the cultural thesis of the good life—be good. But it should not feel good to break twigs. A theme running all through this book is to show how small details are culturally elevated and given symbolic meaning, while other behaviors and events are diminished or concealed. Releasing the ant again after it has been examined under the magnifying glass can therefore be counted as a significant act in preserving animals— just before the children eat hot dogs on the same excursion (Pedersen, 2007). Teaching is imagined as taking place in unproblematic, apolitical situations that do not call for any great sacrifice on the part of the child. Once again, it is the motive that is crucial for the figuration of the eco-certified child, not the effect in saving the environment or protecting animals.

Making Distinctions

Nature as a cultural theses and a place also serves to make a distinction between people. Relating to nature in the "right" way requires a certain cultural competence depending on which nature is concerned, who people are in terms of class, gender, and race, and which activities are intended. This is a theme that is not infrequently seen in both high culture and popular culture, in novels and films, where urban people have to learn to relate to nature in the right way. The movie *Avatar* (Cameron, 2009) is an example of this, where a hopelessly ignorant and insensitive former marine is introduced to the Na'vi people on the planet Pandora. This is a place with wonderfully verdant and magical nature, but it also conceals a precious mineral that people from earth want to get at. The conflict between unspoiled nature and humans' need for growth is the theme of the film, which also affects the way good and evil people are represented (in keeping with the standard Hollywood model). The good individuals are those who live close to nature, and the film follows the learning process of Jake Sully the marine in adapting to this seemingly harmonious life. Through his transformation, and in contrast to his new natural self, the other humans become increasingly evil and brutal in the way they treat animals, nature, and other people. As in almost all fairytales, the categories of good and evil are clearly separated in this type of eco-critical film. A person who acquires the right cultural competence to live in nature can also master it and live in and off it.

The dividing line between those with the right and the wrong nature competence also serves to make distinctions in real life. Children with an immigrant background, living in socially vulnerable suburbs are not infrequently portrayed as needing to get out into the forest. School projects are arranged to move the children to this place for the sake of their development. The report on "Multi-cultural nature" from the governmental organization the Swedish Environmental Protection Agency describes projects of this kind for children and adults (Naturvårdsverket, 2006). In a chapter about school children who get to leave the high-rise buildings in the suburb for a visit to the forest.

This is described as socialization into a more modern "Swedish" way of relating to nature—namely, that it is something to be worshipped and protected—"healing for body and soul" as the historian of ideas Sverker Sörlin puts it in another, more critical chapter in the same book (Naturvårdsverket, 2006, p. 33). Nature is no longer dangerous or an obstacle to people's work, just an opportunity and a place for learning:

> The trial project with the children clearly shows that nature is a good arena in which to learn how to cooperate. Presumably this is because it is a somewhat alien, somewhat frightening environment. Moreover, it is free of the enormous background noise of impressions typical of the urban environment, making it easier for individuals to see each other. (Naturvårdsverket, 2006, p. 49)

In my hometown of Malmö they have started mobile "bus preschools" based in socially stigmatized areas in order to rectify what is often called "these children's" (i.e. poor, immigrant children's) lack of nature and experiences in nature. Likewise, the local government in Malmö has planned and organized a recreation area intended to suit the category of "immigrants." The people stuck together in this cultural category are believed to be uninterested in idyllic experiences of nature, so plans are made instead to utilize the woodland, with fruit trees and the like. It is suggested that the plants should come from the original landscape of "the immigrants" (whatever that might be given that roughly 170 nationalities are represented in the population of Malmö), since the link to an origin is considered important to counter alienation in the face of nature (Naturvårdsverket, 2006, p. 44). The "immigrants" become the Other through the good intention itself and by defining Our attitude to nature as being different from Theirs. Their relation to nature is considered "premodern" and "traditional" (Naturvårdsverket, 2006, pp. 41ff.), compared with a modern Swedish—simultaneously rational and romantic—attitude to nature.

This means that nature also becomes a place where a person—a non-Swede—can learn to acquire "Swedishness." Camilla Safrankova is studying integration projects in Swedish nature (in the singular); vulnerable groups—especially refugees—learn about nature in nature and are thus expected to be enabled to become more "Swedish" (Safrankova & Ideland, 2017). The categories "Swedish" and "knowing about nature" and "nature lovers" stick together and create a foundation stone in the imagined national community that Benedict Anderson (2006) talks of. Making nature and recreation areas more accessible to everyone is of course done with the best of intentions, and it should definitely be encouraged for the sake of equity. The opposite, that natural areas become reserves for the white middle class, is of course frightening and certainly not something to strive for. But once again I must point out that the desire to include also singles out certain people as problems to be solved—and in this inclusion process they are (re)produced as the Other, this time with—to put it in extreme terms—Nature Deficit Disorder. It is the Other who must learn to make use of Swedish nature in a way that is at least relatively Swedish, in order to appear more Swedish, even though they can never pass as fully Swedish. As described above, the forest outing has long been a part of Sweden's nation build-ing and hence also an element in the creation of Swedish identity.

Other kinds of people are positioned in different places and with other activities in nature. In the previous chapter, I discussed how groups are described as being at different stages of "development"—as regards democracy, orderly behavior, and so on—and how differences between different peoples are constituted through these narratives. In the making of Us and Them, however, not all representations of the Other are negative. On the contrary, the Other is often held up as being closer to nature, which is an attribute that can be stuck to people in the sustainability discourse. This is not unproblematic either. Hübinette et al. write:

> Certain minorities can be described as more natural, spiritual, authentic, or unaffected in comparison with white Swedes and Westerners who are thought to have been "spoiled" by life in modern, industrialized, urban societies. This type of exoticizing representations is just as problematic as the openly negative ones, because they also conceal the diversity and variation that can be found in the group being portrayed. (Hübinette, Hörnfeldt, Farahani, & Rosales, 2012, p. 27)

One central aspect in the Othering of so-called traditional countries from so-called civilized countries is the emphasizing of their relative closeness to nature:

> It is often said that we who live in modern communities have come so far from nature that we no longer understand how it works. (*Spektrum Biologi*, 2006, p. 180)

"We"—according to the texts—have been distancing ourselves from nature, while "They" still live closely connected to nature, and have a direct dependence upon the natural world around them. So even positive attributes create distinctions in that people in the North and the South, in the West and the Rest, are (re)produced as Different. Most Different of all are indigenous people, known as *naturfolk* (nature people) in Sweden, and in the following quotation this difference is constructed through several different taken-for-granted assumptions, for example, the difference between those who live close to nature and those who are far removed from it, those who are knowledgeable and capable, those who need help and those who give help (Ideland & Malmberg, 2014):

> In, for example, Ecuador, the Achuara people are now engaged in eco-tourism. Until the 1970's, they lived completely isolated in the rainforest and unaffected by modern civilization. They engaged in felling trees to make room for livestock, but now they get about 45 percent of their income through the eco-village Kapawi, where they are responsible for maintenance and services, and serve as guides on excursions into the rainforest. In 2011, the Achuara people are being counted upon to be able to independently manage the entire eco-village, which will then be donated to them. Hopefully, the village will become a sustainable project for both people and the environment. (Bowden, 2005, p. 31)

Here one can see clear examples of the double gesture of including and excluding (Popkewitz, 2012), particularly by exercising epistemic violence (Spivak, 1988). With help from more civilized people, the Achuara can be included in modern society—which is supposed to lead to sustainability. But in this desire to include, they are also clearly exposed as being different, being the Other whom We can visit in order to come closer to nature. Similar projects can be seen in ecotourist trips to Masai villages in Kenya, allowing Westerners to experience what it is like to live the life of the primitive, and thereby be enriched. But at the same time a clear distinction is made, not least of all concerning who regards whom and in what circumstances people can be considered interesting enough to be regarded. The colonial gaze is highly present in "sustainable" ecotourism. By making distinctions, We in the West also justify acts such as regarding people from the outside, developing and civilizing the Other and simultaneously appearing good. The acts are based on a colonial worldview (Ideland & Malmberg, 2014). Amy Sloane (2012, p. 183) points out that closeness to nature is a possible positive attribute for desirable subjects in environmental education. However, in the Swedish ESE discourse, this attribute sometimes works in the Othering of traditional societies from civilized societies. The notion of nature also includes the notion of who is developed and underdeveloped, those who are technologically advanced as opposed to those lacking the simplest modern facilities such as clean water, electricity, and so forth. The closeness to nature must be played out in a rational way.

Let us return to the discussion of how "nature" is both a place and a metaphor for organizing possible and impossible ways of living and being, and how this place is culturally linked to a specific "type" of kind (Hacking, 2006; Haraway, 2004). This "kind" is impregnated by gender, age, skin color, class, functionality. Those who do not fit in become, in the words of the sociologist Nirmal Puwar (2004), "space invaders," bodies that are made visible because they break the somatic norm. Children are connected to this place. But it is not just any children, it is the eco-certified, natural child that is considerate—but simultaneously dauntless, enjoying while learning and actively playing. A classic ideal image of childhood, to which the Other "space invaders"—who are not positioned in nature but in the urban concrete suburb—must be socialized. In this way, the Others will also develop the rational feeling for nature that appears to be necessary in the work for sustainable development. Nature is not to be used just any old way, as primitive peoples do; it is a modern attitude that is emphasized as the only possible position in nature—and hence it is also modern people (in the Swedish context: knowledgeable, white, Western) that can be defined as belonging to that space; they are not trespassing like space invaders.

Our Common World

Another place that functions in the discourse of sustainability as both a geographical location and a central metaphor that structures the discourse is "our planet"—also called "our common world," "Mother Earth," or even "Gaia." The notion of the earth as our home is a governing technology that is communicated in words and pictures (Ideland & Malmberg, 2015). Maps, photographs, and illustrations of the globe are powerful means of persuasion in the creation of eco-certified individuals. For me personally, a map of the world on the website of the Swedish newspaper *Aftonbladet* in September 2015 struck me to the very soul. Climate researchers were able to demonstrate that the climate had become warmer over almost the whole earth, apart from one spot in the North Atlantic, just south of Iceland and Greenland, which broke the record for cold temperatures. This is caused by melting glaciers, but also by changing circulation in the ocean currents, including the Gulf Stream that is so important for our Scandinavian, relatively mild, climate (Melin, 2015). This map conjured up, at least in my mind, horrific pictures from apocalyptic movies like *The Day after Tomorrow*. Earth as a place served as an effective governing technology.

The historian of technology Sabine Höhler (2015) draws attention to the metaphor of Spaceship Earth as fundamental in the environmental movement. From the 1960s to the 1990s it was used to highlight issues of the earth's resources, the relation between mankind and the planet, and the future. Through new technological possibilities with satellite images, the Cold War fear of nuclear war, and the ecological awakening, the earth was constructed as a shared place, at the same time as modern technology and its potential came into focus. Höhler describes Spaceship Earth as a natural–technological hybrid, that is to say, both its nature and the technology required to understand it entailed a change in the way mankind was positioned in this—very large—place. Humanity as a whole became the population that had to be organized. At the same time as the planet was shrinking and appearing increasingly vulnerable, one can say that people's responsibility and potential to act grew in the cultural awareness. This is best illustrated by the constantly recurring image of the globe held in one or more human hands. The fate of the earth is in the hands of humans, not the other way around. Mankind is pictured as not being dependent on the earth, which—if we think carefully—is a strange metaphor in the environmental movement. Images like this emphasize mankind's potential to act, and they simultaneously obscure the problems that affect people because of pollution, war, floods, famine, and refugee flows. Since humans have possibilities, they are also responsible for their own fate and that of the planet. Neither is there a discussion about different possibilities and responsibilities; the earth is one and so is the humankind. The fate of the earth has been constructed as a shared responsibility, not just for those who bear the guilt for the problems. This also conceals the capitalist systems and the injustices that are actually both the cause and the effect of the devastation of the environment.

The elevation of the metaphorical places Nature and the Planet makes environmental and sustainability work into a "nice" practice. Unpleasant problems and injustices, the economistic and high-tech instruments are all dressed in a soft, almost religious, language and thus help to make the project incontestable. If one were to follow, for instance Naomi Klein's (2015) suggestions about a global restructuring of resources as a consequence of climate change, or if one even mentioned the apparatus of economic success that created the environmental problems in the first place, it would be difficult for the sustainability issue to take root as a nonthreatening, nonpolitical, and conflict-free teaching practice in school. Nor would so many people have been able to identify with the project. No, it feels better just to "hang around in nature" or perhaps "Boil macaroni with birdsong, open landscapes, biological diversity, and unsprayed fields," as in the advertisement for eco-certified products. In this way, you can assume your personal responsibility for the world and stand out as a good—and natural—person with no artificial additives. Even if the global effect is probably minimal.

References

Adlercreutz, O. (2012, August 8). Hundar påverkar klimatet mer än bilar. *Teknikens värld*.

Ahmed, S. (2007). The language of diversity. *Ethnic and Racial Studies, 30*(2), 235–256.

Ahmed, S. (2014). The politics of good feeling. *Critical Race and Whiteness HållStudies, 10*(2), 1–19.

Anderson, B. (2006). *Imagined communities: Reflections on the origin and spread of nationalism*. Brooklyn: Verso Books.

Ärlemalm-Hagsér, E. (2013). *Engagerade i världens bästa? Lärande för hållbarhet i förskolan*. Gothenburg: Gothenburg University. Diss.

Bowden, R. (2005). *Hållbar utveckling: Hotet mot miljön*. Stockholm: Liber.

Braun, T., & Dierkes, P. (2017). Connecting students to nature—How intensity of nature experience and student age influence the success of outdoor education programs. *Environmental Education Research, 23*(7), 937–949.

Byrne, J., Ideland, M., Malmberg, C., & Grace, M. (2014). Climate change and everyday life: Repertoires children use to negotiate a socio-scientific issue. *International Journal of Science Education, 36*(9), 1491–1509.

Cameron, J. (2009). *Avatar*. Fox.

Fletcher, R. (2015). Nature is a nice place to save but I wouldn't want to live there: Environmental education and the ecotourist gaze. *Environmental Education Research, 21*(3), 338–350.

Fletcher, R. (2017). Connection with nature is an oxymoron: A political ecology of "nature-deficit disorder". *The Journal of Environmental Education, 48*(4), 226–233.

Frykman, J., & Löfgren, O. (1987). *Culture builders: A historical anthropology of middle-class life*. New Brunswick: Rutgers University Press.

Hacking, I. (2006). Making up people. *London Review of Books 28*(16), 3–26.

Halldén, G. (Ed.). (2009). *Naturen som symbol för den goda barndomen*. Stockholm: Carlssons.

Håll Sverige Rent. (2011). *Blixtpatrullens äventyr*. Author: L. Adelsköld.

Haraway, D. J. (2004). *The Haraway reader*. New York: Routledge.

Harding, S. (Ed.). (2011). *The postcolonial science and technology studies reader*. Durham: Duke University Press.

Hillbur, P., Ideland, M., & Malmberg, C. (2016). Response and responsibility: Fabrication of the eco-certified citizen in Swedish curricula 1962–2011. *Journal of Curriculum Studies, 48*(3), 409–426.

Hübinette, T., Hörnfeldt, H., Farahani, F., & Rosales, R. L. (2012). *Om ras och vithet i det samtida Sverige*. Tumba: Mångkulturellt centrum.

Höhler, S. (2015). *Spaceship earth in the environmental age, 1960–1990*. London: Pickering & Chatto.

Ideland, M., & Malmberg, C. (2014). Our common world belongs to 'Us': Constructions of otherness in education for sustainable development. *Critical Studies in Education, 55*(3), 369–386.

Ideland, M., & Malmberg, C. (2015). Governing 'eco-certified children' through pastoral power: Critical perspectives on education for sustainable development. *Environmental Education Research, 21*(2), 173–182.

Ideland, M., & Tröhler, D. (2015). Calling for sustainability: WWF's global agenda and educating Swedish exceptionalism. In D. Tröhler & T. Lenz (Eds.), *Trajectories in the development of modern school systems: Between the national and the global* (pp. 199–212). Abingdon and New York: Routledge.

Klein, N. (2014). *This changes everything: Capitalism vs. the climate*. New York: Simon & Schuster.

Klein, N. (2015). *This changes everything: Capitalism vs. the climate*. New York: Simon & Schuster.

Louv, R. (2005). *Last child in the woods: Saving our children from nature-deficit disorder*. Chapel Hill: Algonquin Books.

Louv, R. (2007). Leave no child inside. *Orion Magazine, 57*(11), 1–6.

Löfgren, O. (1997). Mellanrum: Vita fläckar och svarta hål i storstadens utkant. In K. Saltzman & B. Svensson (Eds.), *Moderna landskap*. Stockholm: Natur och Kultur.

Magntorn, O. (2007). *Reading nature: Developing ecological literacy through teaching*. Linköping: Linköping University. Diss.

Mayer, F. S., Frantz, C. M., Bruehlman-Senecal, E., & Dolliver, K. (2009). Why is nature beneficial? The role of connectedness to nature. *Environment and Behavior, 41*(5), 607–643.

McClintock, A. (1995). *Imperial leather: Race, gender and sexuality in the colonial contest*. New York, NY: Routledge.

Melin, E. (2015). Forskare oroade över rekordkallt område. *Aftonbladet, 26*(9), 2015.

Naturvårdsverket. (2006). *Mångnatur: Friluftsliv och natursyn i det mångkulturella samhället.* Stockholm: Naturvårdsverket.

Orr, D. W. (1992). *Ecological literacy: Education and the transition to a postmodern world.* Albany: Suny Press.

Pedersen, H. (2007). *The school and the animal other: An ethnography of human–animal relations in education.* Dissertation, University of Gothenburg, Gothenburg.

Popkewitz, T. S. (2009). Curriculum study, curriculum history, and curriculum theory: The reason of reason. *Journal of Curriculum studies, 41*(3), 301–319.

Popkewitz, T. S. (2012). *Cosmopolitanism and the age of school reform: Science, education, and making society by making the child.* Abingdon and New York: Routledge.

Puwar, N. (2004). *Space invaders, race, gender and bodies out of place.* New York: Berg.

Safrankova, C., & Ideland, M. (2017). *Educational integration projects in Swedish nature—Considerations on space, learning and national identity.* Paper presentation at ECER conference, Copenhagen 22–25 of August, 2017.

Sjöstrand-Öhrfelt, M. (2014). *Barn i natur och natur i barn.* Dissertation, Malmö University, Malmö.

Sloane, A. L. (2012). *On human violence to nature: A philosophical genealogy of environmental education.* Dissertation, University of Wisconsin-Madison, Madison.

Spektrum Biologi. (2006). Stockholm: Liber. Authors: S. Fabricius, F. Holm, & A. Nystrand.

Spivak, G. C. (1988). Can the subaltern speak? In C. Nelson & L. Grossberg (Eds.), *Marxism and the interpretation of culture* (pp. 271–313). Basingstoke, UK: Macmillan Education.

The Royal National Board of Education [Kungliga skolöverstyrelsen]. (1962). *Läroplan för grundskolan* [Curriculum for the compulsory school]. Stockholm: Kungliga skolöverstyrelsen.

Thulin, S. (2011). *Lärares tal och barns nyfikenhet: Kommunikation om naturvetenskapliga innehåll i förskolan.* Dissertation, University of Gothenburg, Gothenburg.

Ting, D. H., Ting, D. H., Cheng, C. F. C., & Cheng, C. F. C. (2017). Developing pro-environmental behaviour: Ecotourism fieldtrip and experiences. *International Journal of Sustainability in Higher Education, 18*(7), 1212–1229.

6

Eco-Certified Children and Irresponsible Adults

Abstract The chapter discusses consequences of individualistic and nationalistic approaches to sustainability and how discourses organize what is seen as reason as well as the reasonable, desirable children who engage in environment and sustainability in a proper way, and consequently also who becomes the eco-certified child's Other. Furthermore, this chapter focuses on how the child is constructed in and through this discourse; how the child becomes the representative for the pure, untouched soul—still not destroyed by the cynicism of the adult world. The figuration of the eco-certified child as an agent of change is problematized. Here I also discuss alternative ways of talking about environment and sustainability, and how other perspectives can redistribute the responsibility for the future from childhood into the political arena.

Keywords Construction of the child · Discourse · Sustainability

One of the first books I read when entering university in the early 1990s was *Culture Builders: A Historical Anthropology of Middle-Class Life* (Frykman & Löfgren, 1987). The book describes how Swedes in the late nineteenth and early twentieth century "learned" how to be

© The Author(s) 2019   **129**
M. Ideland, *The Eco-Certified Child*, Palgrave Studies in Education
and the Environment, https://doi.org/10.1007/978-3-030-00199-5_6

cultured, hygienic, nature-loving, controlled, and modern individuals. Jonas Frykman and Orvar Löfgren help us to understand how this new ideal was integrated in body and mind, regulating the movements and size of bodies and people's behavior and relations. Being clean, exercising emotional self-control, and loving nature became a part of the modern project. This cultured person is close to the figuration of the eco-certified child, who must control both actions and emotions in order to belong to the discourse, and to avoid being dismissed as part of the dangerous population. But could it also be the case that the eco-certified child, just like the cultured person, represents not just a specific environmental discourse but also taken-for-granted cultural notions that recur in other contexts outside ESE and beyond school? The present book, after all, is not just about the environment, sustainable development, and school, but also about two strong political movements of our time: nationalism and individualism.

This book has drawn a somewhat playful picture of the eco-certified child based on criteria we usually see associated with eco-certified food: free-range, natural—with no artificial additives, eco-certified energy, and locally grown. But what began as an amusing play on words has gradually acquired a more serious meaning. Perhaps these criteria not only function for labeling food but also say something more about our society? Are these metaphors that structure our culture in the 2010s and that articulate present-day beliefs about what constitutes good people, good deeds, and good food?

Parallels can be drawn to the American anthropologist Emily Martin's studies of how ideals in society structure our understanding of biological phenomena such as fertilization, the menopause, and the immune system. Among other things, she shows how societal metaphors have ordered our knowledge of the immune system in different times; what might appear to be obvious biological facts are simultaneously a reflection of ideals for the organization of society. Martin has studied a change from the early twentieth-century understanding of the body as a fortress that has to be protected with the aid of walls (hygiene) to war metaphors ("immune defense") during the Cold War. She also interprets the understanding of the human body as a machine that could break down as a fitting metaphor for the increasingly industrialized society.

Flexibility then permeated the late twentieth-century narratives about the body, along with other areas in society. The flexible person—in body and mind—thus becomes the desirable person. The understanding of organization, leadership, workers, politics, school, and so on is also seen in the understanding of the immune system and how a healthy system manages to adapt to different conditions (Martin, 1994).

The way in which biological knowledge is produced and communicated is culturally impregnated; the understanding follows general changes and ideals in society. In the same way, I would argue that the criteria for the eco-certified child, or for eco-certified food for that matter, are more general than the sustainability discourse. The idea of the **free-range** person, making free choices and living a good and—hopefully—rational life, is a cultural thesis that organizes virtually every sphere of life. In Sweden, we are supposed to choose not only specific types of energy and ecological/ordinary tomatoes, but also school, pension fund, telephone company, and so on. It is up to each person to create personal happiness. Also close to this is the idea of **energy**, that you must "do things"; passivity does not count, even if the environmental effect is perhaps the same or better. Moreover, it must be "done" in such a way that it is seen; today's performative sharing culture strengthens the significance of the intention rather than the effect. What is performed is what you are, what is done in secret does not count—for better or worse. This applies to everyday tweeting and face-booking, as well as to corporate brand-building, to say nothing of a researcher's everyday life at university. There performance is measured in the number of published articles rather than the content and effect of the articles. Likewise, nature and the **natural** are acquiring an ever-stronger symbolic value in an increasingly urbanized society where new telephone models are front-page news and nature represents the genuine and the original. Finally, as we all know, nationalist currents are not confined to sustainable development and the idea of national exceptionalism in this field. In a globalized world the local and familiar, the **locally grown**, is significant on many levels—just as happens with the natural in a high-tech society, and so on and so forth.

The cultural thesis of the good life and desirable people, in other words, is not limited to either the educational system or sustainable development and the environment; it also normalizes and pathologizes ways of living in many different societal arenas. Perhaps it is a kind of diagnosis for society as a whole and the notions of the good life and the good citizen. But it also pervades the notion of the good ice cream and other products in which we invest our identity. The (re)production of those who live in the truth and those who need to change recurs in many places, reinforcing the boundaries between those who pass as eco-certified and those who belong to the dangerous population. As I have shown throughout the book, good and responsible is synonymous with a knowledge of science and an interest in nature. The desirable citizen is also able and willing to act and is conscious of the purpose of every action. He or she is also optimistic and positive, full of self-confidence, and last but not least: Swedish (in the Swedish context). And white. The dangerous citizen is one who cannot or will not assume responsibility, lacks knowledge, capacity for action, and engagement in the "right things," feels resigned and/or angry and is somewhere else in the world, with a skin color other than white. In short, people are categorized according to education, economic potential, their voice and position in society, the color of their skin, their nationality and geographical location. The project of education for sustainable development becomes a discourse of distinction through its good intentions to help, foster, and educate. It makes demands of people—especially children—to change their way of life, even though the children who are regarded as dangerous may be the ones with the lowest potential to govern their own lives.

Unchildish Children

In the sustainability discourse children are described, through comparisons with adults, as those who can—and thus should—save the planet. In the teaching material this is of particular significance, since school is the place where future citizens are fostered and children are equipped for the future. To some extent popular culture disseminates a similar message. The film *Tomorrowland* (Bird, 2015), for example, has a child and a teenager who represent hope for the future, while the adult world is cynical. At the same time, the children are positioned not only as future citizens, but also as today's agents of change. Children are given responsibility even in their childhood. As we have seen, this is closely associated with a changed outlook on children in society from citizens in the becoming to responsible societal actora. In a report from the UN-associated organization *OMEP* (Organisation Mondiale pour l'Éducation Préscolaire, in English the World Organization for Early Childhood Education), which works with education for sustainable development, the (global) child is described as follows under the heading "A view on children":

> Children of today are citizens—competent, active agents in their own lives with rights of their own (UN, 1989). They are affected by and capable of engaging with complex environmental and social issues. They steer away from romanticized notions of childhood as an arena for innocent play that positions all children as leading exclusively sheltered, safe and happy lives untouched by events around them. As values, attitudes, behaviours and skills are acquired already during early childhood, this is where ESD has to start. (Engdahl & Rabušicová, 2010, p. 4)

Education for sustainable development should thus proceed from a kind of childhood different from the romanticized childhood filled with innocent play. The starting point is instead the competent child in a complex world—which is also a conception that is materialized in the textbooks, steering documents, games, films, and children's books analyzed above. That children are central figures in children's culture is nothing new or specific to the sustainability discourse. On the contrary, child culture and school culture are Inhabited by children who solve various problems that the adult world seemingly ignores or appears to be incapable of tackling. But even outside the arena of school and children's culture, the competent child stands out through the sustainability discourse. One example is the Swedish electricity company Telge Energi's advertising campaign in recent years. In these advertisements, the child is the one who enlightens the adult world about environmental problems and the solutions to them. One picture shows a small but determined child holding a teddy bear in one hand and using the other to tweak a judge by the ear. The text reads: "Lower the tax on clean electricity!" Another picture shows a notice pinned to a board with a message obviously handwritten by a child: "Daddy switch to clean electricity and I promise to stop asking if we are nearly there yet. Max." Beside is a computer-printed notice: "We cannot place the climate crisis in our children's lap."

In the campaign with letters and notes from children to their parents, the child is at once a childish child and a responsible citizen. With the aid of "childlike" threats such as "repeatedly asking if we are nearly there yet" or "singing all the way until we get there," adults are supposed to be persuaded to buy Telge's electricity to escape the childish behavior of the child. In the sustainable society, the child is rather unchildish, but still retaining the free-thinking, wise, and natural virtues of the child. In the world of advertising these seem to be a "natural" part of the child—also symbolically illustrated with a picture of a newborn baby "giving the finger," with the text: "Haven't changed to solar power yet?"

The child's inherent engagement in sustainability can also be seen in another campaign from Telge, in which posters and television ads illustrate children's stories of what ought to happen to adults who buy dirty electricity, for instance: "eat ice cream in a sandstorm," "live under a storm," "wear winter overalls in the sauna," or "dance cheek-to-cheek with a rotten fish" (Telge Energi, 2015). It is obvious that the child's perspective is put across here, with crazy ideas and suitably harsh punishments. The child is made into the advocate of the good, sustainable lifestyle (Dahlbeck, 2012) and a promise of a better future. This hope, as we have seen, is also a central feature of the sustainability discourse; problems and disasters must be transformed into hopes of happiness and a better world (Ahmed, 2010). This materializes the idea of the competent child that emerged in the late twentieth century, as an alternative to the view of the child as the one who had to be developed on the terms of the adult world.

The competent child is far from being the vulnerable child described, for example, by the historian Finis Dunaway (2015) in his study of American images in the environmental movement. In these pictures the child represents risks rather than solutions. Children's bodies are portrayed as vulnerable, receptive to toxins and other threats. Moreover, the vulnerable children are almost exclusively white in Dunaway's American study (although he says that ethnic minorities are more often exposed to environmental risks). Dunaway points out how the white child becomes the universal vulnerable child, easy to identify within a society permeated by somatic norms of whiteness. In a different historical and national context, Sweden in the 2010s, the white child represents something completely different, namely, competence and capacity to act. The vulnerable child is the child-of color, somewhere else on earth, that the competent white child will help.

Instead of being viewed as an unfinished or more vulnerable version of the adult, the competent child—as we see here—actually takes more responsibility than adults do. The adult becomes the Other, the irresponsible, unnatural, capitalistic, and dishonest. The construction of the eco-certified child becomes even clearer through the construction of the Other in the form of the Teenager. This is the teenager outside school, because within the walls of the educational system teenagers are viewed as possible changers of society, future citizens who must develop useful knowledge. But outside school a traditional image is (re)produced of the lazy, unengaged, wasteful, self-centered teenager, for example in the advertisements from a another electricity company where consumers are encouraged to "Catch home electricity thieves red-handed" (Eon, 2015). The picture shows a brash teenage girl with headphones behind the text "Teenagers consume more electricity than adults." Under her a boy is yawning behind the words "Sifo [a major Swedish market survey company]: Teenagers consume most—and they know they do."

The figurations of the self-centered, lazy teenager, and the cynical adult function as Others in the (re)production of the responsible, altruistic, knowledge-using, natural, and competent child. Through the comparison with other generations (as a cultural category), the eco-certified child emerges, on whose shoulders the problems of the future can be placed. In earlier chapters, I have mentioned the problem of a post-political perspective on sustainability issues, where both conflicts and political solutions are made invisible, instead emphasizing individual solutions, scientific evidence, and objective numbers. In a similar way, the figure of the competent child and the future citizen who will solve the problems is an idea that helps to depoliticize the sustainability issue. The (re)production of eco-certified people—especially children—helps to make it possible, as Naomi Klein (2015) writes, for big companies to go on impacting the environment and the climate with no real political opposition. The political muscles are atrophied when the problems are placed on the shoulders of individual children who, despite their lack of income, suffrage, and established channels for making their voices heard in society, are expected to be able to change the world through rational, individual actions. This means that the possibilities for real change may perhaps disappear.

In other words, the good intention of strengthening children's sense of empowerment and competence to act, and of making them into political actors *additionally* has problematic effects—both for the children themselves of whom the demands are made and for the general conception of how environmental and sustainability problem can and should be solved, and which actions are possible to imagine. Of course this is not the only effect of the belief in the competent and eco-certified child. Other, more positive discursive effects are that children are listened to and taken seriously. Despite this, I have sought to draw attention to the creation of inclusion and exclusion resulting from the good intentions of teaching sustainability. The problems that the sustainability movement actually wants to counteract—hopelessness, inequality, waste of resources—risk being exacerbated.

References

Ahmed, S. (2010). *The promise of happiness.* Durham: Duke University Press.
Bird, B. (2015). *Tomorrowland.* Walt Disney Productions.
Dahlbeck, J. (2012). *On childhood and the good will: Thoughts on ethics and early childhood education.* Malmö: Malmö University.
Dunaway, F. (2015). *Seeing green: The use and abuse of American environmental images.* Chicago: University of Chicago Press.
Engdahl, I., & Rabušicová, M. (2010). *Children's voices about the state of the earth and sustainable development.* Göteborg: OMEP.
Eon. (2015). *Ta hemmets eltjuvar på bar gärning.* Advertisment.

Frykman, J., & Löfgren, O. (1987). *Culture builders: A historical anthropology of middle-class life*. New Brunswick: Rutgers University Press.

Klein, N. (2015). *This changes everything: Capitalism vs. the climate*. Nueva York: Simon & Schuster.

Martin, E. (1994). *Flexible Bodies: The role of immunity in American culture from the days of polio to the age of AIDS*. Boston: Beacon Press.

Telge Energi. (2015). *Advertisments*.

References

Adichie, C. N. (2009). *The danger of a single story*. Ted Talks. http://www.ted.com/talks/chimamanda_adichie_the_danger_of_a_single_story?language=en.

Adlercreutz, O. (2012, August 8). Hundar påverkar klimatet mer än bilar. *Teknikens värld*.

Ahmed, S. (2004). Affective economies. *Social Text, 22*(2), 117–139.

Ahmed, S. (2007). The language of diversity. *Ethnic and Racial Studies, 30*(2), 235–256.

Ahmed, S. (2010). *The promise of happiness*. Durham: Duke University Press.

Ahmed, S. (2012a). Whiteness and the general will: Diversity work as willful work. *Philosophia, 2*(1), 1–20.

Ahmed, S. (2012b). *On being included: Racism and diversity in institutional life*. Durham and London: Duke University Press.

Ahmed, S. (2014a). *The cultural politics of emotion* (2nd ed.). Edinburgh: Edinburgh University Press.

Ahmed, S. (2014b). The politics of good feeling. *Critical Race and Whiteness Studies, 10*(2), 1–19.

Almers, E. (2009). *Handlingskompetens för hållbar utveckling: Tre berättelser om vägen dit*. Jönköping: Högskolan för lärande och kommunikation.

© The Editor(s) (if applicable) and The Author(s), under exclusive licence to Springer Nature Switzerland AG 2019
M. Ideland, *The Eco-Certified Child*, Palgrave Studies in Education and the Environment, https://doi.org/10.1007/978-3-030-00199-5

Anderson, B. (2006). *Imagined communities: Reflections on the origin and spread of nationalism*. Brooklyn: Verso Books.

Andersson, P. (2018). Business as un-usual through dislocatory moments— Change for sustainability and scope for subjectivity in classroom practice. *Environmental Education Research, 24*(5), 648–662.

Andrée, M., Hansson, L., & Ideland, M. (2018). Political agendas and actors in science teaching: An analysis of teaching materials from NGOs and private companies. In A. Arvola-Orlander, K. Othrell-Cass, & M. K. Sillasen (Eds.), *Cultural, social, and political perspectives in science education* (pp. 75–92). Cham: Springer.

Arendt, H. (1963). *Eichmann in Jerusalem: A report on the banality of evil*. New York, NY: Penguin.

Ärlemalm-Hagsér, E. (2013). *Engagerade i världens bästa? Lärande för hållbarhet i förskolan*. Gothenburg: Gothenburg University. Diss.

Ball, S. J. (2009). Privatising education, privatising education policy, privatising educational research: Network governance and the 'competition state'. *Journal of Education Policy, 24*(1), 83–99.

Bartholdsson, Å. (2014). Narrating anger: Conceptualisations and representations of children's anger in programmes for social and emotional learning. *Power and Education, 6*(3), 295–306.

Bauman, Z. (1996). *Postmodern etik*. Göteborg: Daidalos.

Bengtsson, S., & Östman, L. (2013). Globalisation and education for sustainable development: Emancipation from context and meaning. *Environmental Education Research, 19*(4), 477–498.

Bennett, J. (2001). *The enchantment of modern life: Attachments, crossings, and ethics*. Princeton, NJ: Princeton University Press.

Bernstein, B. (2001). From pedagogies to knowledge. In A. Morals, I. Neves, B. Davies, & H. Daniels (Eds.), *Towards a sociology of pedagogy: The contribution of Basil Bernstein to research*. New York: Peter Lang.

Billig, M. (1999). Conversation analysis and the claims of naivety. *Discourse & Society, 10*(4), 572–576.

Bird, B. (2015). *Tomorrowland*. Walt Disney Productions.

Björneloo, I. (2012). Handlingskompetens på schemat. In K. Rönnerman (Ed.), *Aktionsforskning i praktiken – förskola och skola på vetenskaplig grund*. Studentlitteratur: Lund.

Bonilla-Silva, E. (2003). 'New racism,' color-blind racism, and the future of Whiteness in America. In A.W. Doane & E. Bonilla-Silva, (Eds.), *White* out: *The continuing significance of racism* (pp. 271–284). New York and London: Routledge.

Börjesson, M., & Palmblad, E. (2003). *I problembarnens tid: Förnuftets moraliska ordning*. Stockholm: Carlssons.

Bourdieu, P. (1986). The forms of capital. In I. Szeman & T. Kaposy (Eds.), *Cultural theory: An anthology* (pp. 81–93). Chichester: Blackwell.

Bowden, R. (2005). *Hållbar utveckling: Hotet mot miljön*. Stockholm: Liber.

Bradley, K. (2009). *Just environments: Politicising sustainable urban development*. Stockholm: KTH.

Braun, T., & Dierkes, P. (2017). Connecting students to nature—How intensity of nature experience and student age influence the success of outdoor education programs. *Environmental Education Research, 23*(7), 937–949.

Breiting, S., Mayer, M., & Mogensen, F. (2005). "Quality criteria for ESD-schools". *Guidelines to enhance the quality of education for sustainable development*. Vienna: Austrian Federal Ministry of Education, Science, and Culture.

Breiting, S., Hedegaard, K., Mogensen, F., Nielsen, K., & Schnack, K. (2009). *Action competence, conflicting interests and environmental education—The MUVIN Programme*. Odense: Odense Universitetsforlag.

Brembeck, H., Johansson, B., & Kampmann, J. (2004). Introduction. In H. Brembeck, B. Johansson, & J. Kampmann (Eds.), *Beyond the competent child: Exploring contemporary childhoods in the Nordic welfare societies* (pp. 7–32). Fredriksberg: Roskilde University Press.

Brown, W. (2006). *Regulating aversion: Tolerance in the age of identity and empire*. Princeton, NJ: Princeton University Press.

Burman, E. (2009). Beyond 'emotional literacy' in feminist and educational research. *British Educational Research Journal, 35*(1), 137–155.

Butler, J. (1993). *Bodies that matter: On the discursive limits of 'sex'*. New York, NY: Routledge.

Byrne, J., Ideland, M., Malmberg, C., & Grace, M. (2014). Climate change and everyday life: Repertoires children use to negotiate a socio-scientific issue. *International Journal of Science Education, 36*(9), 1491–1509.

Cachelin, A., Rose, J., & Paisley, K. (2015). Disrupting neoliberal discourse in critical sustainability education: A qualitative analysis of intentional language framing. *Environmental Education Research, 21*(8), 1127–1142.

Cameron, J. (2009). *Avatar*. Fox.

Carter, R. G. (2006). Of things said and unsaid: Power, archival silences, and power in silence. *Archivaria, 61,* 215–233.

Castañeda, C. (2002). *Figurations: Child, bodies, worlds*. Durham: Duke University Press.

Castro-Gómez, S. (2002). The social sciences, epistemic violence, and the problem of the "invention of the other". *Nepantla: Views from South, 3*(2), 269–285.

Child, L. (2008). *Hjälp vår jord*. Stockholm: Rabén & Sjögren.

Cooke, A. N., Fielding, K. S., & Louis, W. R. (2016). Environmentally active people: The role of autonomy, relatedness, competence and self-determined motivation. *Environmental Education Research, 22*(5), 631–657.

Cowen, R. (2014). With the exception of Switzerland … thoughts about the nation and educational research. *IJHE Bildungsgeschichte 4*(2), 216–228.

Dahlbeck, J. (2012). *On childhood and the good will: Thoughts on ethics and early childhood education*. Malmö: Malmö University.

Dahlstedt, M. (2010). Hårda nypor för ett mjukt samhälle? Om medialisering och rasifiering i utspelspolitikens Sverige. *Sociologisk Forskning, 47*(3), 35–56.

Douglas, M. (1966/2002). *Purity and danger: An analysis of concepts of pollution and taboo*. London: Taylor & Francis.

Dunaway, F. (2015). *Seeing green: The use and abuse of American environmental images*. Chicago: University of Chicago Press.

Dyer, R. (1993). The matter of images. *Essays on representations*. New York, NY: Routledge.

Dyer, R. (1997). *White*. New York, NY: Routledge.

Edmondson, B. (2014). *Ice cream social: The struggle for the Soul of Ben & Jerry's*. San Fransisco: Berrett-Koehler.

Ellergard, T. (2004). Self-governance and incompetence: Teachers' construction of "the competent child". In H. Brembeck, B. Johansson, & J. Kampmann (Eds.), *Beyond the competent child: Exploring contemporary childhoods in the Nordic welfare societies* (pp. 177–198). Fredriksberg: Roskilde University Press.

Elmqvist, A. (1970/2012). *Sprätten satt på toaletten*. Stockholm: Karneval förlag.

Emmerich, R. (2004). *The day after tomorrow*. Twentieth Century Fox.

Engdahl, I., & Rabušicová, M. (2010). *Children's voices about the state of the earth and sustainable development*. Göteborg: OMEP.

Eon. (2015). *Ta hemmets eltjuvar på bar gärning*. Advertisment.

Essed, P. (1991). *Understanding everyday racism: An interdisciplinary theory*. Newbury Park, CA: Sage.

Fletcher, R. (2015). Nature is a nice place to save but I wouldn't want to live there: Environmental education and the ecotourist gaze. *Environmental Education Research, 21*(3), 338–350.

Fletcher, R. (2017). Connection with nature is an oxymoron: A political ecology of "nature-deficit disorder". *The Journal of Environmental Education, 48*(4), 226–233.

Foucault, M. (1971). *Orders of discourse: Social science information, 10*(2), 7–30.

Foucault, M. (1980). *Power/knowledge: Selected interviews and other writings 1972–1977* (C. Gordon, Ed.). Harlow: Harvester Press.

Foucault, M. (1983). The subject and power. In H. Dreyfus & P. Rabinow (Eds.), *Michel Foucault: Beyond structuralism and hermeneutics* (pp. 208–226). Chicago, IL: University of Chicago Press.

Foucault, M. (1990). *The History of Sexuality*, vol. 1. New York: Vintage Books.

Foucault, M. (1991). Governmentality. In G. Burchell, C. Gordon, & P. Miller (Eds.), *The Foucault effect: Studies in governmentality* (pp. 87–104). Chicago, IL: University of Chicago Press.

Foucault, M., Senellart, M., & Davidson, A. I. (2007). *Security, territory, population*. Basingstoke: Palgrave Macmillan.

Foucault, M., Ewald, F., & Fontana, A. (2010). *The birth of biopolitics: Lectures at the Collège de France, 1978–1979* (M. Senellart, Ed.). New York: Palgrave Macmillan.

Fröhlich, G., Sellmann, D., & Bogner, F. X. (2013). The influence of situational emotions on the intention for sustainable consumer behaviour in a student-centred intervention. *Environmental Education Research, 19*(6), 747–764.

Frykman, J., & Löfgren, O. (1987). *Culture builders: A historical anthropology of middle-class life*. New Brunswick: Rutgers University Press.

Gagen, E. A. (2013). Governing emotions: Citizenship, neuroscience and the education of youth. *Transactions of the Institute of British Geographers, 40*, 140–152.

González-Gaudiano, E. (2005). Education for sustainable development: Configuration and meaning. *Policy Futures in Education, 3*(3), 243–250.

Gore, A. (2006). *An inconvenient truth*. Paramount Pictures.

Gorur, R. (2014). Towards a sociology of measurement in education policy. *European Educational Research Journal, 13*(1), 58–72.

Gottlieb, D., Vigoda-Gadot, E., & Haim, A. (2013). Encouraging ecological behaviors among students by using the ecological footprint as an educational tool: A quasi-experimental design in a public high school in the city of Haifa. *Environmental Education Research, 19*(6), 844–863.

Gough, N. (2002). Thinking/acting locally/globally: Western science and environmental education in a global knowledge economy. *International Journal of Science Education, 24*(11), 1217–1237.

Gough, A. (2006). A long, winding (and rocky) road to environmental education for sustainability in 2006. *Australian Journal of Environmental Education, 22*(1), 71–76.

Gough, S., & Scott, W. (2006). Education and sustainable development: A political analysis. *Educational Review, 58*(3), 273–290.

Greenpeace. (2014). *LEGO: Everything is NOT awesome.* Retrieved April 7, 2016, from https://www.youtube.com/watch?v=qhbliUq0_r4.

Grek, S. (2009). Governing by numbers: The PISA 'effect' in Europe. *Journal of Education Policy, 24*(1), 23–37.

Hacking, I. (1995). The looping effects of human kinds. *Causal cognition: A multidisciplinary debate, 12,* 351–394.

Hacking, I. (2006). Making up people. *London Review of Books 28*(16), 3–26.

Håkansson, M., Östman, L., & Van Poeck, K. (2018). The political tendency in environmental and sustainability education. *European Educational Research Journal, 17*(1), 91–111.

Hall, S. (1992). The west and the rest: Discourse and power. In S. Hall & B. Geiben (Eds.), *Formations of modernity* (pp. 15–30). Cambridge, UK: Polity Press.

Håll Sverige Rent. (2008). *Mofflor och människor.* Author: L. Petri.

Håll Sverige Rent. (2011). *Blixtpatrullens äventyr.* Author: L. Adelsköld.

Halldén, G. (Ed.). (2009). *Naturen som symbol för den goda barndomen.* Stockholm: Carlssons.

Haraway, D. J. (2004). *The Haraway reader.* New York: Routledge.

Haraway, D. J. (2016). *Staying with the trouble: Making kin in the Chthulucene.* Durham: Duke University Press.

Harding, S. (Ed.). (2011). *The postcolonial science and technology studies reader.* Durham: Duke University Press.

Hasslöf, H. (2015). *The educational challenge in "education for sustainable development": Qualification, social change and the political.* Malmö: Malmö University. Diss.

Hertzberg, F. (2015). Double gestures of inclusion and exclusion: Notions of learning outcomes, autonomy, and informed choices in Swedish educational and vocational guidance. *International Journal of Qualitative Studies in Education, 28*(10), 1203–1228.

Heyck, H. (2012). Producing reason. In M. Solovey & H. Cravens (Eds.), *Cold war social science: Knowledge production, liberal democracy, and human nature* (pp. 99–116). New York: Palgrave Macmillan.

Hillbur, P., Ideland, M., & Malmberg, C. (2016). Response and responsibility: Fabrication of the eco-certified citizen in Swedish curricula 1962–2011. *Journal of Curriculum Studies, 48*(3), 409–426.

Hobson, J. M. (2004). *The Eastern origins of Western civilisation.* Cambridge: Cambridge University Press.

Höhler, S. (2015). *Spaceship earth in the environmental age, 1960–1990.* London: Pickering & Chatto.

Holmberg, T., & Ideland, M. (2016). Imagination laboratory: Making sense of bio-objects in contemporary genetic art. *Sociological Review, 64*(3), 447–467.

http://data.footprintnetwork.org/#/. Retrieved June 29, 2018.

http://www.greenpeace.org/sweden/se. Retrieved June 3, 2015.

http://www.greenpeace.org. Retrieved June 3, 2015.

http://www.svanen.se/radda-varlden/. Retrieved June 8, 2015.

https://en.unesco.org/themes/education-sustainable-development/what-is-esd/un-decade-of-esd. Retrieved June 3, 2015.

http://www.youthxchange.net. Retrieved June 3, 2015.

Hübinette, T. (2014). Racial stereotypes and Swedish antiracism: A Swedish crisis of multiculturalism? In L. Jensen & K. Loftsdóttir (Eds.), *Crisis in the Nordic nations and beyond: At the intersection of environment, finance and multiculturalism* (pp. 69–85). Farnham: Ashgate.

Hübinette, T., & Lundström, C. (2011). Sweden after the recent election: The double-binding power of Swedish whiteness through the mourning of the loss of 'old Sweden' and the passing of 'good Sweden'. *NORA—Nordic Journal of Feminist and Gender Research, 19*(1), 42–52.

Hübinette, T., Hörnfeldt, H., Farahani, F., & Rosales, R. L. (2012). *Om ras och vithet i det samtida Sverige.* Tumba: Mångkulturellt centrum.

Hultqvist, K., & Dahlberg, G. (Eds.). (2001). *Governing the child in the new millennium.* Sussex, UK: Psychology Press.

Hursh, D., Henderson, J., & Greenwood, D. (2015). Environmental education in a neoliberal climate. *Environmental Education Research, 21*(3), 299–318.

Iconosquare.com/tag/batterijakten. Retrieved June 5, 2015.

Ideland, M. (2014). How PISA becomes transformed into a Nationalistic Project: Reflections upon a Swedish 'school crisis'. *IJHE Bildungsgeschichte, 4*(2), 243–245.

Ideland, M., & Malmberg, C. (2014). Our common world belongs to 'Us': Constructions of otherness in education for sustainable development. *Critical Studies in Education, 55*(3), 369–386.

Ideland, M., & Malmberg, C. (2015). Governing 'eco-certified children' through pastoral power: Critical perspectives on education for sustainable development. *Environmental Education Research, 21*(2), 173–182.

Ideland, M., & Tröhler, D. (2015). Calling for sustainability: WWF's global agenda and educating Swedish exceptionalism. In D. Tröhler & T. Lenz (Eds.), *Trajectories in the development of modern school systems: Between the national and the global* (pp. 199–212). Abingdon and New York: Routledge.

Ideland, M. (2016). The action-competent child: Responsibilization through practices and emotions in environmental education. *Knowledge Cultures, 4*(2), 95–112.

Ideland, M. (2017). The end of the world and a promise of happiness: Environmental education within the cultural politics of emotions. In T. Popkewitz, J. Diaz, & C. Kirchgasler (Eds.), *A political sociology of educational knowledge: Studies of exclusions and difference.* London: Taylor & Francis.

Ideland, M. (in press). *Science, coloniality and "the great rationality divide". How practices, places and persons are culturally attached to each other in science education.* https://doi.org/10.1007/s11191-018-0006-8

Jensen, B. B., & Schnack, K. (2006). The action competence approach in environmental education. *Environmental Education Research, 12*(3–4), 471–486.

Jickling, B., & Wals, A. E. (2008). Globalization and environmental education: Looking beyond sustainable development. *Journal of Curriculum Studies, 40*(1), 1–21.

Johansson, B. (2004). Consumption and ethics in a children's magazine. In H. Brembeck, B. Johansson, & J. Kampmann (Eds.), *Beyond the competent child: Exploring contemporary childhoods in the Nordic welfare societies* (pp. 229–250). Fredriksberg: Roskilde University Press.

Kampmann, J. (2004a). Det selv-i-agt-tagelige barn. *Psyke & Logos, 25*(2), 21.

Kampmann, J. (2004b). Societalization of childhood: New opportunities? New demands? In H. Brembeck, B. Johansson, & J. Kampmann (Eds.), *Beyond the competent child: Exploring contemporary childhoods in the Nordic welfare societies* (pp. 127–152). Fredriksberg: Roskilde University Press.

Kenway, J., & Youdell, D. (2011). The emotional geographies of education: Beginning a conversation. *Emotion, Space and Society, 4*(3), 131–136.

Klein, N. (2015). *This changes everything: Capitalism vs. the climate.* New York: Simon & Schuster.

Knutsson, B. (2013). Swedish environmental and sustainability education research in the era of post-politics? *Utbildning & Demokrati 22*(2), 105–122.

Kopnina, H. (2012). Education for sustainable development (ESD): The turn away from 'environment'in environmental education? *Environmental Education Research, 18*(5), 699–717.

Kopnina, H., & Cherniak, B. (2016). Neoliberalism and justice in education for sustainable development: A call for inclusive pluralism. *Environmental Education Research, 22*(6), 827–841.

Kramming, K. (2017). *Miljökollaps eller hållbar framtid?: Hur gymnasieungdomar uttrycker sig om miljöfrågor.* Uppsala: Uppsala University. Diss.

Kulick, D. (2005). The importance of what gets left out. *Discourse Studies, 7*(4–5), 615–624.

Kunskapsförlaget. (2015). Retrieved June 5, 2015, from http://kunskapsförlaget.se/DAGENS-MILJÖNYHETER/[PID/7/M/NewsV2/Action/1/NewsId/87]/Talande-ord.aspx.

Ladson-Billings, G. (1998). Just what is critical race theory and what's it doing in a nice field like education? *International Journal of Qualitative Studies in Education, 11*(1), 7–24.

Latour, B. (1993). *We have never been modern.* Cambridge: Harvard University Press.

Lazzarato, M. (2010). Pastoral power: Beyond public and private. *Open, 19,* 18–32.

Lin, S. M. (2016). Reducing students' carbon footprints using personal carbon footprint management system based on environmental behavioural theory and persuasive technology. *Environmental Education Research, 22*(5), 658–682.

Lloro-Bidart, T. (2017). Neoliberal and disciplinary environmentality and 'sustainable seafood' consumption: Storying environmentally responsible action. *Environmental Education Research, 23*(8), 1182–1199.

Lotz-Sisitka, H., Wals, A. E., Kronlid, D., & McGarry, D. (2015). Transformative, transgressive social learning: Rethinking higher education pedagogy in times of systemic global dysfunction. *Current Opinion in Environmental Sustainability, 16,* 73–80.

Louv, R. (2005). *Last child in the woods: Saving our children from nature-deficit disorder.* Chapel Hill: Algonquin Books.

Louv, R. (2007). Leave no child inside. *Orion Magazine, 57*(11), 1–6.

Luke, T. W. (1999). Environmentality as green governmentality. In E. Darier (Ed.), *Discourses of the environment* (pp. 121–151). Malden, MA: Blackwell.

Lundahl, L. (2002). From centralisation to decentralisation: Governance of education in Sweden. *European Educational Research Journal, 1*(4), 625–636.

Löfgren, O. (1997). Mellanrum: Vita fläckar och svarta hål i storstadens utkant. In K. Saltzman & B. Svensson (Eds.), *Moderna landskap*. Stockholm: Natur och Kultur.

Magntorn, O. (2007). *Reading nature: Developing ecological literacy through teaching*. Linköping: Linköping University. Diss.

Manni, A., Sporre, K., & Ottander, C. (2017). Emotions and values—A case study of meaning-making in ESE. *Environmental Education Research, 23*(4), 451–464.

Mannion, G., Biesta, G., Priestley, M., & Ross, H. (2011). The global dimension in education and education for global citizenship: Genealogy and critique. *Globalisation, Societies and Education, 9*(3–4), 443–456.

Marcus, G. E. (1995). Ethnography in/of the world system: The emergence of multi-sited ethnography. *Annual Review of Anthropology, 24*(1), 95–117.

Martin, E. (1994). *Flexible bodies: The role of immunity in American culture from the days of polio to the age of AIDS*. Boston: Beacon Press.

Matias, C. E., & Zembylas, M. (2014). 'When saying you care is not really caring': Emotions of disgust, whiteness ideology, and teacher education. *Critical Studies in Education, 55*(3), 319–337.

Mayer, F. S., Frantz, C. M., Bruehlman-Senecal, E., & Dolliver, K. (2009). Why is nature beneficial? The role of connectedness to nature. *Environment and Behavior, 41*(5), 607–643.

McClintock, A. (1995). *Imperial leather: Race, gender and sexuality in the colonial contest*. New York, NY: Routledge.

McElhinny, B. (2010). The audacity of affect: Gender, race, and history in linguistic accounts of legitimacy and belonging. *Annual Review of Anthropology, 39*, 309–328.

McKenzie, M. (2012). Education for y'all: Global neoliberalism and the case for a politics of scale in sustainability education policy. *Policy Futures in Education, 10*(2), 165–177.

McKenzie, M., Bieler, A., & McNeil, R. (2015). Education policy mobility: Reimagining sustainability in neoliberal times. *Environmental Education Research, 21*(3), 319–337.

Melin, E. (2015). Forskare oroade över rekordkallt område. *Aftonbladet, 26*(9), 2015.

Miller, P. (2004). Governing by numbers: Why calculative practices matter. In A. Amin & N. Thrift (Eds.), *The Blackwell cultural economy reader.* Oxford: Blackwell.

Miller, P., & Rose, N. (2008). *Governing the present.* Cambridge: Polity Press.

Mouffe, C. (2011). *On the political.* Abingdon: Routledge.

Nadesan, M. H. (2010). *Governing childhood into the 21st century: Biopolitical technologies of childhood management and education.* New York: Palgrave Macmillan.

National Agency for Education [Skolverket]. (2011). *Curriculum for the compulsory school, preschool class and the recreation centre 2011.* Stockholm: Swedish National Agency for Education.

Naturskyddsföreningen. (2013). *Energifallet.* Retrieved June 5, 2015 from http://www.scribd.com/doc/122751716/Energifallet.

Naturvårdsverket. (2006). *Mångnatur: Friluftsliv och natursyn i det mångkulturella samhället.* Stockholm: Naturvårdsverket.

Nordvall, H., & Dahlstedt, M. (2009). Folkbildning i (av)koloniseringens skugga: Demokrati, nationella mytologier och solidaritetens paradoxer. *Utbildning och Demokrati, 18*(3), 29–47.

Öhman, J. (2006). Pluralism and criticism in environmental education and education for sustainable development: A practical understanding. *Environmental Education Research, 12*(2), 149–163.

Ojala, M. (2013). Emotional awareness: On the importance of including emotional aspects in education for sustainable development (ESD). *Journal of Education for Sustainable Development, 7*(2), 167–182.

Ojala, M. (2015). Hope in the face of climate change: Associations with environmental engagement and student perceptions of teachers' emotion communication style and future orientation. *The Journal of Environmental Education, 46*(3), 133–148.

Olmedo, A., Bailey, P. L., & Ball, S. J. (2013). To infinity and beyond…: Heterarchical governance, the teach for all network in Europe and the making of profits and minds. *European Educational Research Journal, 12*(4), 492–512.

Orr, D. W. (1992). *Ecological literacy: Education and the transition to a postmodern world.* Albany: Suny Press.

Östman, L., Svanberg, S., & Aaro-Östman, E. (2013). *From vision to lesson: Education for sustainable development in practice.* Stockholm, Sweden: WWF.

Otieno, C., Spada, H., Liebler, K., Ludemann, T., Deil, U., & Renkl, A. (2014). Informing about climate change and invasive species: How the presentation of information affects perception of risk, emotions, and learning. *Environmental Education Research, 20*(5), 612–638.

Palmer, J. A. (1998). *Environmental education in the 21st century: Theory, practice, progress and promise.* London: Routledge.

Pedersen, H. (2007). *The school and the animal other: An ethnography of human–animal relations in education.* Dissertation, University of Gothenburg, Gothenburg.

Persson, M., Sjöström, B., & Johnsson, P. (2007). *Klimatsmart: Din guide till en miljövänligare vardag.* Stockholm: Alfabeta.

Popkewitz, T. S. (1998). *Struggling for the soul: The politics of schooling and the construction of the teacher.* New York: Teachers College Press.

Popkewitz, T. S. (2004). The alchemy of the mathematics curriculum: Inscriptions and fabrications of the child. *American Educational Journal, 41*(4), 3–34.

Popkewitz, T. S. (2009a). Curriculum study, curriculum history, and curriculum theory: The reason of reason. *Journal of Curriculum studies, 41*(3), 301–319.

Popkewitz, T. (2009b). Globalization as a system of reason: The historical possibility and the political in pedagogical policy and research. *Yearbook of the National Society for the Study of Education, 108*(2), 247–267.

Popkewitz, T. (2011). PISA. In M. A. Pereyra, H. G. Kotthoff, & R. Cowen (Eds.), *PISA under examination: Changing knowledge, changing tests, and changing schools.* Rotterdam: Sense Publishers.

Popkewitz, T. S. (2012). *Cosmopolitanism and the age of school reform: Science, education, and making society by making the child.* Abingdon and New York: Routledge.

Popkewitz, T. S., & Lindblad, S. (2004). Historicizing the future: Educational reform, systems of reason, and the making of children who are the future citizens. *Journal of Educational Change, 5*(3), 229–247.

Pred, A. (2000). *Even in Sweden: Racisms, racialized spaces, and the popular geographical imagination.* Berkeley: University of California Press.

Pripp, O., & Öhlander, M. (2012). Att uppfatta rasism i Sverige. Om glassreklam och normstrider. In T. Hübinette, H. Hörnfeldt, F. Farahani, & R. L. Rosales (Eds.), *Om ras och vithet i det samtida Sverige.* Tumba: Mångkulturellt centrum.

Puwar, N. (2004). *Space invaders, race, gender and bodies out of place.* New York: Berg.

Richardson, L., & St. Pierre, E. (2008). A method of inquiry. *Collecting and Interpreting Qualitative Materials, 3*(4), 473.

Rittel, H. W. J., & Webber, M. M. (1973). Dilemmas in a general theory of planning. *Policy Sciences, 4*, 155–169.

Rizvi, F., & Lingard, B. (2010). *Globalizing education policy*. London: Routledge.

Rose, N. (1991). Governing by numbers: Figuring out democracy. *Accounting, Organizations and Society, 16*(7), 673–692.

Rose, N. (1998). *Inventing our selves: Psychology, power, and personhood.* Cambridge: Cambridge University Press.

Rose, N., & Miller, P. (2010). Political power beyond the state: Problematics of government. *The British Journal of Sociology, 61*, 271–303.

Safrankova, C., & Ideland, M. (2017). *Educational integration projects in Swedish nature—Considerations on space, learning and national identity.* Paper presentation at ECER conference, Copenhagen 22–25 of August, 2017.

Sahlberg, P. (2011). The fourth way of Finland. *Journal of Educational Change, 12*(2), 173–185.

Said, E. (1978). *Orientalism: Western representations of the Orient.* New York: Pantheon.

Schwarzenbach, A. (2011). *Saving the world's wildlife: WWF—The first 50 years.* London, UK: Profile.

Sellar, S. (2015). A feel for numbers: Affect, data and education policy. *Critical Studies in Education, 56*(1), 131–146.

Serder, M., & Ideland, M. (2016). PISA truth effects: The construction of low performance. *Discourse: Studies in the Cultural Politics of Education, 37*(3), 341–357.

Seth, S. (2009). Putting knowledge in its place: Science, colonialism, and the postcolonial. *Postcolonial Studies, 12*(4), 373–388.

Simons, M., & Masschelein, J. (2008). The governmentalization of learning and the assemblage of a learning apparatus. *Educational Theory, 58*(4), 391–415.

Sjöstrand-Öhrfelt, M. (2014). *Barn i natur och natur i barn.* Dissertation, Malmö University, Malmö.

Skolverket. (1994), *Läroplan för det obligatoriska skolväsendet, förskoleklassen och fritidshemmet Lpo 94.* Stockholm: Skolverket.

Skolverket. (2011). *Läroplan för grundskolan, förskoleklassen och fritidshemmet 2011.* Stockholm: Skolverket.

Skolöverstyrelsen. (1969). *Läroplan för grundskolan.* Stockholm: Svenska utbildningsförlaget Liber.

Skolöverstyrelsen. (1980). *Läroplan för grundskolan, Lgr 80.* Stockholm: Liber.

Sloane, A. L. (2012). *On human violence to nature: A philosophical genealogy of environmental education.* Dissertation, University of Wisconsin-Madison, Madison.

Soneryd, L., & Uggla, Y. (2015). Green governmentality and responsibilization: New forms of governance and responses to 'consumer responsibility'. *Environmental Politics, 24*(6), 913–931.

SO.S Geografi. (2012). Stockholm: Liber. Authors: L. Lindberg & S. Mårtensson.

SO.S Samhälle. (2012). Stockholm: Liber. Authors: U. Andersson, P. Ewert, & U. Hedengren.

Spektrum Biologi. (2006). Stockholm: Liber. Authors: S. Fabricius, F. Holm, & A. Nystrand.

Spivak, G. C. (1988). Can the subaltern speak? In C. Nelson & L. Grossberg (Eds.), *Marxism and the Interpretation of Culture* (pp. 271–313). Basingstoke, UK: Macmillan Education.

Svenskt näringsliv. (2010). *Miljö – så funkar det.* Stockholm: Svenskt näringsliv.

Telge Energi. (2015). *Advertisments.*

The Royal National board of Education [Kungliga skolöverstyrelsen]. (1962). *Läroplan för grundskolan* [Curriculum for the compulsory school]. Stockholm: Kungliga skolöverstyrelsen.

Thulin, S. (2011). *Lärares tal och barns nyfikenhet: Kommunikation om naturvetenskapliga innehåll i förskolan.* Dissertation, University of Gothenburg, Gothenburg.

Ting, D. H., Ting, D. H., Cheng, C. F. C., & Cheng, C. F. C. (2017). Developing pro-environmental behaviour: Ecotourism fieldtrip and experiences. *International Journal of Sustainability in Higher Education, 18*(7), 1212–1229.

Tröhler, D. (2009). Harmonizing the educational globe: World polity, cultural features, and the challenges to educational research. *Studies in Philosophy and Education, 29*(1), 7–29.

Tröhler, D. (2011). *Languages of education: Protestant legacies, national identities, and global aspirations.* New York: Routledge.

Typhina, E. (2017). Urban park design+ love for nature: Interventions for visitor experiences and social networking. *Environmental Education Research, 23*(8), 1169–1181.

UN. (1972). *Declaration of the United Nations conference on the human environment.* New York: United Nations.

UN. (1987). *Report of the World Commission on Environment and Development: Our common future.* New York: United Nations.

UN. (1992). *Agenda 21.* New York: United Nations.

Van Poeck, K., Goeminne, G., & Vandenabeele, J. (2016). Revisiting the democratic paradox of environmental and sustainability education: Sustainability issues as matters of concern. *Environmental Education Research, 22*(6), 806–826.

Van Poeck, K., & Östman, L. (2017). Creating space for 'the political' in environmental and sustainability education practice: A political move analysis of educators' actions. *Environmental Education Research*, 1–18. https://doi.org/10.1080/13504622.2017.1306835.

Villenas, S. A., & Angeles, S. L. (2013). Race talk and school equity in local print media: The discursive flexibility of whiteness and the promise of race-conscious talk. *Discourse: Studies in the Cultural Politics of Education, 34*(4), 510–530.

Weber, M. (2009). *From Max Weber: Essays in sociology.* Abingdon: Routledge.

Witoszek, N. (2018). Teaching sustainability in Norway, China and Ghana: Challenges to the UN programme. *Environmental Education Research, 24*(6), 831–844.

WWF. (2010). *Skola på hållbar väg – skolors arbete inom hållbar utveckling.* Solna: WWF.

WWF. (2012). *Förskolan: För en hållbar framtid.* Av: Margareta Lakén. Solna: WWF.

WWF. (2014). *A collection of articles, ideas and links for lesson planning?* Retrieved May 5, 2014, from http://wwf.panda.org/about_our_earth/teacher_resources/.

www.minplanet.se. Retrieved May 5, 2013.

Ygeman, A., & Schönström, A. (2015). Ingenting är mer osvenskt än att se ner på en annan människa på grund av dennes religion eller hudfärg. *Sydsvenskan, 3*(6), 2015.

YouthXChange. (2015). *Ice-cream with a mission.* Retrieved October 9, 2015, from http://www.youthxchange.net/main/benandjerry.asp.

Index